Women's Voices

Women's Voices

A DOCUMENTARY HISTORY OF WOMEN IN AMERICA

VOLUME 1:
Education
Abolition
Suffrage

Edited by Lorie Jenkins McElroy

U·X·L®
AN IMPRINT OF GALE

DETROIT · NEW YORK · TORONTO · LONDON

Women's Voices:
A Documentary History of Women in America

Lorie Jenkins McElroy, Editor

Staff

Elizabeth Des Chenes, *U·X·L Developmental Editor*
Carol DeKane Nagel, *U·X·L Managing Editor*
Thomas L. Romig, *U·X·L Publisher*

Kim Smilay, *Permissions Specialist*

Shanna P. Heilveil, *Production Assistant*
Evi Seoud, *Assistant Production Manager*
Mary Beth Trimper, *Production Director*

Pamela A. E. Galbreath, *Art Director*
Cynthia Baldwin, *Product Design Manager*

Linda Mahoney, *Typesetting*

Library of Congress Cataloging-in-Publication Data

Women's Voices : a documentary history of women in America
/ edited by Lorie Jenkins McElroy
p.   cm.
Includes bibliographical references and index.

Contents: v. 1. Education, abolition, suffrage – v. 2. Equality, property, reproduction

ISBN 0-7876-0663-4 (set: acid-free paper). – ISBN 0-7876-0664-2 (v. 1: acid-free paper). – ISBN 0-7876-0665-0 (v. 2: acid-free paper)

1. Women–United States–History–Sources. 2. Women's Rights–United States–History–Sources. I. McElroy, Lorie Jenkins.

HQ1410.W688   1996
305.4'0973–dc20

96-25579

CIP

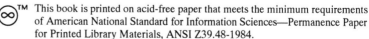 This book is printed on acid-free paper that meets the minimum requirements of American National Standard for Information Sciences—Permanence Paper for Printed Library Materials, ANSI Z39.48-1984.

Printed in the United States of America

10 9 8 7 6 5 4 3 2 1

Contents

__Bold type__ indicates volume number
Regular type indicates page number

Lucretia Mott

Reader's Guide

Women's Voices: A Documentary History of Women in America presents 32 original documents that trace the development of women's rights in America from the Revolutionary War to the present. The speeches, diary entries, newspaper articles, poems, and reminiscences featured in these two volumes explore a number of movements that influenced the crusade for equal rights, including education and labor reform, social equality, and women's suffrage. Activists such as Susan B. Anthony and Sojourner Truth and their works may be recognizable to readers; perhaps less familiar are figures such as Sarah Bagley, who wrote about female workers during the early days of the Industrial Revolution, and Alice Paul, who proposed the first Equal Rights Amendment in 1923. While the majority of entries reflect a feminine perspective, prominent male supporters of women's rights—such as Frederick Douglass—are also represented. In studying the original documents presented in *Women's Voices,* users can gain a unique perspective of how individuals—many of whom risked a great deal to present their views—helped shape the past and influence the present.

Frances E. Willard

Format

Both *Women's Voices* volumes are divided into three chapters. Each of the six chapters focus on a specific theme: Education, Abolition, Suffrage, Labor, Social Equality, and Reproductive Rights. Every chapter opens with an historical overview, followed by four to seven document excerpts.

Each excerpt is divided into six sections:

- **Introductory material** places the document and its author in an historical context
- **Things to Remember** offers readers important background information about the featured text
- **Excerpt** presents the document in its original language and format
- **What happened next** discusses the impact of the document on both the speaker and his or her audience
- **Did you know** provides interesting facts about each document and its author
- **For Further Reading** presents sources for more information on documents and speakers

Additional Features

Every *Women's Voices* entry contains a speaker's biographical box, call-out boxes examining related events and issues, and black-and-white illustrations. Each excerpt is accompanied by a glossary running alongside the primary document that defines terms and ideas. Both volumes contain a timeline of important events and cumulative index.

Acknowledgments

Special thanks are due for the invaluable comments and suggestions provided by U·X·L's women's books advisors:

Annette Haley, High School Librarian/Media Specialist at Grosse Ile High School in Grosse Ile, Michigan; Mary Ruthsdotter, Projects Director of the National Women's History Project; Francine Stampnitzky, Children's/Young Adult Librarian at the Elmont Public Library in Elmont, New York; and Ruth Ann

Karlin Yeske, Librarian at North Middle School in Rapid City, South Dakota.

Thanks also go to the Butler Library at Columbia University, the collections staff at Barnard College and Rutgers University, the reference librarians in Union, New Jersey, and researcher Donald Sauvigne. Added acknowledgment goes to Mary Bell, Robert Frauenhoff, and Lynn Mandon at Wayne Hills High School in Wayne, New Jersey.

Comments and Suggestions

We welcome your comments and suggestions for documents to feature in future editions of *Women's Voices*. Please write: Editor, *Women's Voices,* U·X·L, 835 Penobscot Bldg., Detroit, Michigan, 48226-4094; call toll free: 1-800-347-4253; or fax: 313-961-6348.

Preface

Charlotte Perkins Gilman

When we learn about history from a biography or textbook, our understanding of events and people is colored by an historian's interpretation of the past. When we read primary source documents such as the 32 pieces found in *Women's Voices,* however, we can interpret history for ourselves. The accounts and perspectives in these speeches, diaries, essays, and letters open a unique and very personal window on the past, reminding us that we all make history a little bit every day.

The entries in *Women's Voices* show that women have long shaped historical events (even when their personal stories were written in invisible ink). Through reviewing these primary sources in their historical context, readers discover the vital role American women played in the ongoing fight for equal rights, a fight that often took heavy personal tolls. Readers will learn about the hopes and dreams women held for their families, communities, and country and how these dreams helped shape current social and political trends. The women featured in *Voices* come from differing time periods, backgrounds, and social spheres, yet they are joined by a common bond: the desire to improve the status of *all* women through a variety of means, including education, political activism, and legal reform.

The *Voices* documents—presented whenever possible in their original format—reveal that there was often disagreement about how change should (and would) come about. In some cases, major philosophical differences turned woman against woman; in other instances, unexpected alliances were formed, some of which included men. Many of the women featured in *Voices* saw frustratingly little progress towards equality during their lifetimes—most, in fact, were widely criticized for speaking their minds. While change was slow, progress was eventually made—especially with regard to women's suffrage. Women in today's America have a greater voice than in any period of the country's history. For this, they can thank their predecessors who, through the strength of their own words and beliefs, created a climate where change could be realized.

Mary Ruthsdotter, Projects Coordinator
National Women's History Project
May, 1996

Education

Mary Wollstonecraft

ducation was one of the first areas in which women made strides in their fight for equal rights. In America the idea of equality in education gained vocal support during the Revolutionary War. Encouraged by the fledgling nation's emphasis on personal liberties, women began to speak out about the need for all people—male and female—to have well-rounded educations. One such woman was **Judith Sargent Murray**. Murray, who was largely self-educated, argued that a lack of formal education was the only real factor keeping women from intellectual achievement.

For most girls during Murray's time, education was limited to learning reading and writing at local elementary schools. Teachers and parents encouraged young boys to study more varied subjects and to attend public school for a much longer period of time than their female counterparts. Wealthy families provided private tutoring at home for sons and, in some cases, allowed their daughters to learn by "sitting-in" as their brothers received lessons. Daughters of middle-class families sometimes took lessons from their father, a minister, or other mentor. But for many young women, especially those living in poor rural areas or working in the booming factory towns, the only option for learning consisted of self-education through extensive reading or studying with a group of peers. In the southern states most slaveowners did not allow children born into slavery to receive an education. White family members or adult slaves frequently risked punishment by secretly teaching black children how to read and write.

Englishwoman **Mary Wollstonecraft**, another participant in the public debate concerning women's right to education, helped inspire later generations of women to fight for the right to vote and to gain full civil rights. In 1792 Wollstonecraft echoed Murray's sentiments in the controversial and widely read book *A Vindication of the Rights of Woman*. Largely self-educated, Wollstonecraft supported herself by running a private school in England. Although influenced by the ideals of the French Revolution (1789-99), she objected to the French proposal for public education because of its unequal treatment of young boys and girls. Wollstonecraft vehemently opposed the recommendation that girls stop attending school after the age of eight to stay at home and focus on domestic skills. Due to her influential book, which won international acclaim, Wollstonecraft remains a key figure in the founding of the women's rights movement.

In both the United States and Europe, seminaries offered another form of education to female students. These private schools featured subjects considered appropriate for "proper" young women, such as music, needlework, and dance. Some teachers, such as **Emma Willard**, sought to expand the scope of female seminary education. Willard, founder of the Troy Female Seminary, was one of the first educators to propose a standardized course of study for young women that included philosophy and science.

Not all progressive instructors favored radical change, however. Conservative movement and Hartford Female Seminary founder **Catherine Beecher** felt that a woman's primary concern should be the welfare of her home and family. To this end, Beecher's school offered a course of study that emphasized domestic subjects such as cooking, infant care, and family health. In addition to her role in the development of domestic science, Beecher contributed significantly to the evolving educational system as America expanded into western territories. She urged other women to become teachers because, in her opinion, the teaching profession ideally suited women's natural talents to nurture others. As teachers, women could help shape the destiny of the rapidly growing country.

The work of writers and educators like Willard and Beecher helped establish the groundwork for educational reform. But these changes were slow in coming. During the eighteenth and nineteenth centuries, many women had to abandon their educations in order to help support their families. Young black women were denied even limited access to education until the middle of the nineteenth century, when northern states began to outlaw slavery. In fact, black women and men did not fully receive the right to equal education until the Supreme Court's decision in *Brown vs. Board of Education* in 1954. By striking down the "separate but equal" clause—a principle that legalized segregation in U.S. public schools—the Supreme Court guaranteed that students of all races have equal access to public education.

Even in the late 1990s, though, the concept of "separate but equal" was still being applied on the basis of gender in some educational institutions. As recently as 1996 the Citadel, an all-male military college, claimed that it did not have to admit female cadets if similar military training could be provided at another institution.

By the dawn of the twenty-first century—due in large part to the pioneering efforts of people like Murray, Wollstonecraft, Willard, and Beecher—women *generally* had the same educational opportunities as men. Where once female education seemed unnecessary, modern public and private educational systems embraced students of both genders. In fact, the Education Act of 1972 requires that all American colleges and universities receiving state or federal funding provide students with equal opportunity to education and programs, regardless of gender, race, disability, or other circumstance.

On the Equality of the Sexes

Written by Judith Sargent Murray
Published in Massachusetts Magazine,
March-April 1790

The changes brought about by the American Revolution helped transform the lives of many women. Feeling a new sense of liberty and empowerment, they gained an understanding of their potential for contributing to the young republic. For the first time, women found themselves entering the political arena through various protest-related activities. One such politically active woman was Judith Sargent Murray.

Murray grew up in Gloucester, Massachusetts, in a prominent family deeply involved in the colonial war for independence from Great Britain. Atypical of the time, she was self-educated in writing and acadmeics (efforts encouraged by her father). Her intellectual independence was strengthened after her family's conversion to Universalism (an eighteenth-century Christian-based religion centered on the belief that all people could be saved), which led to criticism from their neighbors and colleagues.

During the Revolutionary War era, the concepts of liberty and human rights were widely discussed. There was also

increasing awareness about the importance of education for the people in a developing young nation. These ideas influenced Murray profoundly. She began to challenge the accepted beliefs concerning women's status in society and to question the lack of educational opportunities. In 1779 she wrote an essay promoting education for women entitled "On the Equality of the Sexes." Murray believed the revolutionary philosophy expressed in the Declaration of Independence—that "all men are created equal"—included women as well. She states in her essay that women have certain natural rights, including the right to be educated. Murray argues against the idea that men are intellectually superior to women and suggests that any differences in thinking between the sexes are due to differences in educational training. In addition to promoting the benefits of a liberal education for women, Murray stresses the importance of traditional roles for women as wives and mothers.

The Sargent House museum in Gloucester, Massachusetts.

Things to Remember While Reading "On the Equality of the Sexes":

- Murray argues that men and women are born with equal mental abilities and that women's minds become inferior due to the poor quality of education they receive compared to men.

- She believes that society, not nature, forces women to focus solely on domestic, or home-related, activities. She further notes that society actually condemns an educated woman.

- Murray also dismisses the idea that since men are physically stronger, they must also have stronger intellectual powers. During her time, many people believed women had weaker or smaller minds than men.

- Notice her use of Old English where "th" replaces "s" at the end of words. For example, "has" is written as *hath* and "does" is written as *doth*.

On the Equality of the Sexes

Is it upon mature consideration we adopt the idea, that nature is thus partial in her distributions? Is it indeed a fact, that she hath yielded to one half of the human species so unquestionable a mental superiority?... Yet it may be questioned, from what doth this superiority, in thus discriminating faculty of the soul, proceed. May we not trace its source in the difference of education, and continued advantages? Will it be said that the judgment of a male of two years old, is more **sage** *than that of a female's of the same age? I believe the reverse is generally observed to be true. But from that period what partiality! how is the one exalted and the other depressed, by the contrary modes of education which are adopted! the one is taught to aspire, and the other is early confined and limited. As their years increase, the sister must be* **wholly domesticated,** *while the brother is led by the hand through all the* **flowery** *paths of science. Grant that their minds are by nature equal, yet who*

Sage: Wise.
Wholly: Completely, totally.
Domesticated: Taught to take care of household, or domestic, needs.
Flowery: Full of fancy words and phrases.

*shall wonder at the apparent superiority, if indeed custom becomes second nature; nay if it taketh place of nature, and that it doth the experience of each day will **evince.** At length arrived at womanhood, the uncultivated fair one feels a void, which the employments **allotted** her are by no means capable of filling. What can she do? to books, she may not apply; or if she doth, to those only of the **novel** kind, lest she merit the **appellation** of a learned lady; and what ideas have been affixed to this term, the observation of many can testify. Fashion, scandal and sometimes what is still more **reprehensible,** are then called in to her relief; and who can say to what lengths the liberties she takes may proceed. Meantime she herself is most unhappy; she feels the want of a cultivated mind. Is she single, she in vain seeks to fill up time from sexual employments or amusements. Is she united to a person whose soul nature made equal to her own, education hath set him so far above her, that in those entertainments which are productive of such rational **felicity,** she is not qualified to accompany him. She experiences a **mortifying** consciousness of inferiority, which embitters every enjoyment. Doth the person to whom her adverse fate hath **consigned** her, possess a mind incapable of improvement, she is equally **wretched**, in being so closely connected with an individual whom she cannot but despise. Now, [if she were] permitted the same instructors as her brother ... for the employment of a rational mind an ample field would be opened. In astronomy she might catch a glimpse of the immensity of the **Deity,** and thence she would form amazing conceptions of the **august** and supreme Intelligence. In geography she would admire Jehova in the midst of his benevolence; thus adapting this globe to the various wants and amusements of its inhabitants. In natural philosophy she would adore the infinite majesty of heaven, clothed in **condescension**; and as she traversed the reptile world, she would hail the goodness of a creating God. A mind, thus filled, would have little room for the **trifles** with which our sex are, with too much justice, accused of amusing themselves, and they would thus be rendered fit companions for those, who should one day wear*

Evince: Show.

Allotted: Assigned.

Novel: Stories, or fiction, about human experiences.

Appellation: Name.

Reprehensible: Deserving blame.

Felicity: Something that causes happiness.

Mortifying: To subject to embarrassment or cause shame.

Consigned: Under the care of another person, in this case a husband.

Wretched: Miserable.

Deity: God.

August: Marked by dignity and magnificence.

Condescension: Acting superior.

Trifles: Something of little value or importance.

The Education Act of 1972 (Title IX)

Title IX requires all colleges and universities that receive state or federal funding to provide equal opportunity to education and programs regardless of gender, race, disability, or other circumstance. For most colleges in the United States, complying with this law is not particularly difficult; coeducation has been the rule among institutions of higher learning since the establishment of the state college system, which dates back to the Land Grant Act of 1862. It wasn't until the early 1980s, however, that the most prestigious Ivy League colleges, as well as the United States Service Academies (Military, Naval, Air Force, Coast Guard, and Merchant Marine), opened their doors to women.

them as their crown.... I would calmly ask, is it reasonable, that a candidate for immortality, for the joys of heaven, an intelligent being, who is to spend an eternity in contemplating the works of Deity, should at present be so degraded, as to be allowed no other ideas, than those which are suggested by the mechanism of a pudding, or the sewing of the seams of a garment? Pity that all such **censurers** of female improvement do not go one step further, and deny their future existence; to be consistent they surely ought.

Yes, ye lordly, ye **haughty** sex, our souls are by nature equal to yours; the same breath of God animates, enlivens, and invigorates us; and that we are not fallen lower than yourselves, let those witness who have greatly towered above the various discouragements by which they have been so heavily oppressed; and though I am unacquainted with the list of celebrated characters on either side, yet from the observations I have made in the contracted circle in which I have moved, I dare confidently believe, that from the commencement of time to the present day, there hath been as many females, as males, who, by the mere force of natural powers, have merited the crown of applause; who thus unassisted, have seized the wreath of fame. I know there are [those] who assert, that as the

Censurers: Critics.
Haughty: Overly proud; scorning.

animal powers of the one sex are superiour, of course their mental faculties also must be stronger; thus attributing strength of mind to the transient organization of this earth born **tenement.** But if this reasoning is just, man must be content to yield the palm to many of the brute creation, since by not a few of his brethren of the field, he is far surpassed in bodily strength. Moreover, was this argument admitted, it would prove too much, for **occular** demonstration evinceth, that there are many robust masculine ladies, and effeminate gentlemen. Yet I fancy that Mr. Pope [Alexander Pope, an English poet who suffered from poor health and curvature of the spine. He is best remembered for his biting satire], though clogged with an **enervated** body, and distinguished by a **diminutive** stature, could nevertheless lay claim to greatness of soul; and perhaps there are many other instances which might be **adduced** to combat so unphilosophical an opinion. Do we not often see, that when the clay built **tabernacle** is well **nigh** dissolved, when it is just ready to mingle with the parent soil, the immortal inhabitant aspires to, and even attaineth heights the most **sublime**, and which were before wholly unexplored. Besides, were we to grant that animal strength proved anything, taking into consideration the accustomed impartiality of nature, we should be induced to imagine, that she had invested the female mind with superiour strength as an equivalent for the bodily powers of man. But waving this however **palpable** advantage, for equality only, we wish to contend. (Rossi, pp. 18-22)

What happened next...

Murray's notes suggest she wrote "On the Equality of the Sexes" as early as 1779 but did not publish it until 1790. According to this timeline, her ideas on the need for equal educational opportunities for women predate the famous work of British intellectual and writer Mary Wollstonecraft by more than a

Tenement: Housing or dwelling.

Occular (spelled today as "ocular"): Seen by the eye.

Enervated: Weakened.

Diminutive: Small size.

Adduced: Offered as argument or proof.

Tabernacle: A house or place of worship.

Nigh: Close; near.

Sublime: Inspirational; supreme.

Palpable: Obvious.

Judith Sargent Murray

Judith Sargent Murray (1751-1820) was born in Gloucester, Massachusetts, to a prominent family with ties to the shipping trade. She was educated in domestic skills and taught herself to read and write. Murray married John Stevens, a merchant and sea captain, when she was 18 years old; she began writing in her twenties. After being widowed, she married her pastor, John Murray, with whom she had two children. In addition to writing numerous essays for popular magazines, Murray penned plays and published several books. In her later years she lived in Natchez, Mississippi, with her daughter.

dozen years. It is possible that Murray decided to publish her essay in the *Massachusetts Magazine* when the works of other revolutionary writers, such as Wollstonecraft, began to appear in both British and American journals in the late 1780s.

For many years Murray continued to write about gender bias in education in her popular magazine column *The Gleaner*. (A *gleaner* is someone who collects things little by little.) She covered a wide variety of topics and used many different writing styles, including the question-and-answer format, which later became very popular in American journalism.

Did you know...

- Murray used the pseudonym, or pen name, *Constantia* so that her magazine essays would be viewed independently from her husband, John Murray, who was a famous Universalist minister.

- Murray is perhaps best known for *The Gleaner,* a series of essays that was published as a three-volume book in 1798 with a dedication to President John Adams. This series is regarded as an important literary work because of its relevance to the burgeoning young nation.

- Murray was the first native-born American woman dramatist to have her plays professionally performed.

For Further Reading

Rossi, Alice S., ed. *The Feminist Papers: From Adams to de Beauvoir.* New York: Columbia University Press, 1973.

Solomon, Barbara Miller. *In the Company of Educated Women: A History of Women and Higher Education in America.* New Haven, Connecticut: Yale University Press, 1985.

Under, Harlow. *American Profiles: Teachers and Educators.* New York: Facts on File, 1994.

A Vindication of the Rights of Woman

Written by Mary Wollstonecraft
Published in 1792

In 1792 London-born writer and teacher Mary Wollstonecraft published her views concerning women's education and social status in *A Vindication of the Rights of Woman.* Her book, which was reprinted in Philadelphia and Boston, created heated debate in both Great Britain and the United States. Wollstonecraft was the first writer to speak with forceful conviction against the unequal educational opportunities offered to women; she quickly caught the public's attention. Today Wollstonecraft is regarded by many as the founder of the women's rights movement.

Greatly influenced by the struggle for liberty that fueled the French Revolution (1789-1799), Wollstonecraft wrote *A Vindication* in response to a proposal for national education under the new French constitution. The proposal recommended that girls receive the same public education as boys until the age of eight, when girls were then expected to stay home and focus on domestic skills. Based on her own experiences as a teacher, Wollstonecraft was in an excellent position to respond to the

William Blake illustrated Wollstonecraft's 1788 collection entitled Original Stories.

French plan. She had established a school of her own and had also written a collection of essays titled *Thoughts on the Education of Daughters.*

Wollstonecraft criticized popular male writers who stressed the importance of "ladylike" behavior among women. While her writing was filled with exaggerations to make her point (known as *polemics,*) she delivered a compelling message that struck a chord with both fans and opponents. Wollstonecraft urged American society to lift restrictions on women's roles and to offer them an education equal to that afforded men. Only then, she believed, would women's status in society improve.

Things to Remember While Reading *A Vindication of the Rights of Woman*:

- Wollstonecraft claims that men and women are, in fact, born equal, but the way women are raised in society makes them seem inferior to men. Since men and women are fundamentally equal, she argues that they should receive identical educations.

- She emphasizes the importance of a strong mind and a strong body and suggests a program of physical education for women.

- Notice that Wollstonecraft implies that men themselves are degraded, or corrupted, by the inferiority forced on women. She speculates that an end to the oppression of women will greatly improve society overall.

A Vindication of the Rights of Woman

*I have turned over various books written on the subject of education, and patiently observed the conduct of parents and the management of schools; but what has been the result?—a profound conviction that the neglected education of my fellow-creatures is the grand source of the misery I deplore; and that women, in particular, are rendered weak and wretched by a variety of concurring causes, originating from one hasty conclusion. The conduct and manners of women, in fact, evidently prove that their minds are not in a healthy state; for, like the flowers which are planted in too rich a soil, strength and usefulness are sacrificed to beauty; and the **flaunting** leaves, after having pleased a **fastidious** eye, fade, disregarded on the*

Flaunting: To flutter; to show off.

Fastidious: Extremely difficult to please.

stalk, long before the season when they ought to have arrived at maturity. One cause of this barren blooming I attribute to a false system of education, gathered from the books written on this subject by men who, considering females rather as women than human creatures, have been more anxious to make them alluring mistresses than affectionate wives and rational mothers; and the understanding of the sex has been so **bubbled** by this **specious homage,** that the civilized women of the present century, with a few exceptions, are only anxious to inspire love, when they ought to cherish a nobler ambition, and by their abilities and virtues exact respect....

Yet, because I am a woman, I would not lead my readers to suppose that I mean violently to **agitate** the contested question respecting the quality or inferiority of the sex; but as the subject lies in my way, and I cannot pass it over without subjecting the main tendency of my reasoning to misconstruction, I shall stop a moment to deliver, in a few words, my opinion. In the government of the physical world it is observable that the female in point of strength is, in general, inferior to the male. This is the law of nature; and it does not appear to be suspended or **abrogated** in favour of woman. A degree of physical superiority cannot, therefore, be denied—and it is a noble **prerogative**! But not content with this natural **pre-eminence,** men endeavour to sink us still lower, merely to render us alluring objects for a moment; and women, intoxicated by the adoration which men, under the influence of their senses, pay them, do not seek to obtain a durable interest in their hearts, or to become the friends of the fellow creatures who find amusement in their society.

I am aware of an obvious inference:—from every quarter have I heard exclamations against masculine women; but where are they to be found? If by this **appellation** men mean to **inveigh** against their **ardour** in hunting, shooting, and gaming, I shall most cordially join in the cry; but if it be against the imitation of manly virtues, or, more properly speaking, the attainment of those talents and virtues, the exercise of which

Bubbled: *Made useless.*
Specious: *Seeming to be correct but not really so.*
Homage: *Honor or respect shown publicly.*
Agitate: *To stir up interest.*
Abrogated: *Abolished or ended by authority.*
Prerogative: *Exclusive right or privilege.*
Pre-eminence: *Superiority.*
Appellation: *Name or title.*
Inveigh: *To protest bitterly.*
Ardour (spelled today as "ardor"): *Strong enthusiasm.*

ennobles the human character, and which raise females in the scale of animal being, when they are comprehensively termed mankind;—all those who view them with a **philosophic** eye must, I should think, wish with me, that they may every day grow more and more masculine....

I earnestly wish to point out in what true dignity and human happiness consists—I wish to persuade women to endeavour to acquire strength, both of mind and body, and to convince them that the soft phrases, susceptibility of heart, delicacy of sentiment, and refinement of taste, are almost synonymous with **epithets** of weakness, and that those beings who are only the objects of pity and that kind of love, which has been termed its sister, will soon become objects of contempt.

Dismissing, then, those pretty feminine phrases, which the men **condescendingly** use to soften our slavish dependence, and despising that weak elegancy of mind, exquisite sensibility, and sweet **docility** of manners, supposed to be the sexual characteristics of the weaker **vessel,** I wish to [show] that elegance is inferior to virtue, that the first object of **laudable** ambition is to obtain a character as a human being, regardless of the distinction of sex; and that secondary views should be brought to this simple **touchstone**....

The education of women has, of late, been more **attended** to than formerly; yet they are still reckoned a frivolous sex, and ridiculed or pitied by the writers who endeavour by satire or instruction to improve them. It is acknowledged that they spend many of the first years of their lives in acquiring a **smattering** of accomplishments; meanwhile strength of body and mind are sacrificed to **libertine** notions of beauty, to the desire of establishing themselves,—the only way women can rise in the world,—by marriage. And this desire making mere animals of them, when they marry they act as such children may be expected to act:—they dress; they paint, and nickname God's creatures. Surely these weak beings are only fit, for a **seraglio!**—Can they be expected to govern a family

Ennobles: To elevate or make noble.

Philosophic: Wise.

Epithets: Descriptive words or terms.

Condescendingly: Acting in a superior way.

Docility: Being easily taught; submissive.

Vessel: A person regarded as holding or containing some quality.

Laudable: Praiseworthy.

Touchstone: A test or standard of quality.

Attended: Paid attention.

Smattering: Small or scattered amount.

Libertine: Without morals.

Seraglio: Harem.

with judgment, or take care of the poor babes whom they bring into the world?

If then it can be fairly deduced from the present conduct of the sex, from the prevalent fondness for pleasure which takes place of ambition and those nobler passions that open and enlarge the soul; that the instruction which women have hitherto received has only tended, with the constitution of civil society, to render them insignificant objects of desire—mere **propagators** of fools!—if it can be proved that in aiming to accomplish them, without cultivating their understandings, they are taken out of their sphere of duties, and made ridiculous and useless when the short-lived bloom of beauty is over, I presume that rational men will excuse me for endeavouring to persuade them to become more masculine and respectable.

Indeed the word masculine is only a **bugbear**: there is little reason to fear that women will acquire too much courage or **fortitude;** for their apparent inferiority with respect to bodily strength, must render them, in some degree, dependent on men in the various relations of life; but why should it be increased by prejudices that give a sex to virtue, and **confound** simple truths with sensual **reveries?**

Women are, in fact, so much degraded by mistaken notions of female excellence, that I do not mean to add a **paradox** when I assert, that this artificial weakness produces a **propensity** to **tyrannnize**, and gives birth to cunning, the natural opponent of strength, which leads them to play off those contemptible **infantine** airs that undermine esteem even whilst they excite desire. Let men become more **chaste** and modest, and if women do not grow wiser in the same ratio, it will be clear that they have weaker understandings. It seems scarcely necessary to say, that I now speak of the sex in general. Many individuals have more sense than their male relatives; and, as nothing **preponderates** where there is a constant struggle for an equilibrium, without it has naturally more gravity, some women govern their husbands without degrading themselves, because intellect will always govern. (Wollstonecraft, pp. 31-36)

Propagator: Someone who causes something to reproduce or spread.

Bugbear: Dreaded thing; goblin.

Fortitude: Strength of mind that allows someone to bear danger or adversity.

Confound: Baffle.

Reveries: Daydreams.

Paradox: A statement that seems contradictory yet may be true.

Propensity: A tendency.

Tyrannnize (spelled today as "tyrannize"): To rule with unjust severity.

Infantine: Immature, childish.

Chaste: Morally pure in conduct and thoughts.

Preponderates: To be greater in power, force, or weight.

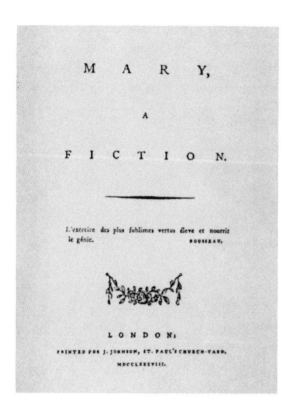

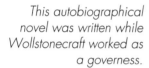

This autobiographical novel was written while Wollstonecraft worked as a governess.

What happened next...

Most members of British society in the early 1790s objected to a woman writing with the frankness, or directness, of Wollstonecraft. The author was widely criticized in the press in the form of satire, or sarcastic essays, which attacked her views. But Wollstonecraft had her own group of admirers and enjoyed much fame and financial security due to the success of her controversial book.

Wollstonecraft left London in 1792, the same year she published *A Vindication of the Rights of Woman.* She settled in Paris so she could witness the French Revolution firsthand. Returning to England in 1795, she became active in a leading radical group of intellectuals that included British political reformer William Godwin, American Revolutionary leader Thomas Paine, and poets William Blake and William Wordsworth. In 1797 she married Godwin. That same year, at the age of 38, Wollstonecraft died giving birth to their daughter, Mary.

Did you know...

- When she was 28 years old, Wollstonecraft learned German and Italian and began to work as a translator and reviewer for a magazine.

- She also voiced her ideas concerning the upbringing of boys and girls in a collection of stories for children called *Original Stories,* published in 1788.

- Wollstonecraft's daughter, Mary Wollstonecraft Shelley, wrote the famous novel *Frankenstein* in 1818.

- Almost one hundred years after *A Vindication,* Elizabeth Cady Stanton placed Wollstonecraft at the top of the list of women to whom she dedicated *History of Woman Suffrage.*

Mary Wollstonecraft

Mary Wollstonecraft (1759-1797) was born in London, England. She educated herself at home under the guidance of her close friend Fanny Blood and then co-established a fairly successful school. To help pay the rent for the school building, Wollstonecraft published her first work, a collection of essays titled *Thoughts on the Education of Daughters.* She married British political reformer William Godwin in 1797 and died the same year during childbirth. Nearly two decades later, the couple's daughter, Mary, married the poet Percy Bysshe Shelley.

For Further Reading

Rossi, Alice S., ed. *The Feminist Papers: From Adams to de Beauvoir.* New York: Columbia University Press, 1973.

Wollstonecraft, Mary. *A Vindication of the Rights of Woman.* Edited by Charles W. Hagelman, Jr. New York: W. W. Norton, 1967.

An Address to the Public Proposing a Plan for Improving Female Education

Presented by Emma Willard
New York State Legislature
Albany, New York, 1819

In the early 1800s young girls living in New England generally received some amount of free elementary education at town schools. Prosperous families could also send their daughters to private secondary schools known as female seminaries, or academies. At the time most people believed women should only concern themselves with finding a husband, raising a family, and managing a household, so the female academies had little reason to teach subjects typically offered at all-male schools. In addition, women were actually thought to have smaller or weaker mental capacities than men. Female academies only taught those subjects considered suitable for a young lady, such as embroidery, painting, singing, French, and music. While some of these schools provided adequate lessons by experienced teachers, many were poorly managed.

Emma Willard was the first educator who realized that the prejudices concerning women's abilities to learn could only be overcome by a more standardized course of study. As one of the earliest advocates of equality in women's education, Willard devoted her life to improving education for women and training teachers for the growing nationwide system of public schools. Her efforts helped establish high schools for girls, women's colleges, and coeducational universities.

Willard served as a principal of a girls' academy in 1807 and then opened her own boarding school for girls in 1814. She was an excellent teacher who worked hard to find ways to teach important and difficult subjects to her eager students. Willard's experiences led her to develop a plan for a state-sponsored institution of higher learning for women. Her goal was to create a school that would teach young girls natural philosophy, or science, as well as domestic skills. In 1819 she outlined her plan in *An Address to the Public; Particularly to the Members of the Legislature of New-York, Proposing a Plan for Improving Female Education.* Willard organized her ideas into four sections: she explained why most young girls in the United States did not receive secondary education after elementary school; she outlined the principles by which education should be regulated; she sketched her ideas for a female seminary; and, in summation, she described in great detail the benefits society would receive from such seminaries.

Willard traveled to Albany to propose her plan to the New York state legislature. However, since it was not considered proper for a woman to appear publicly before male officials, she had to meet with the legislators individually to discuss her recommendations.

Things to Remember While Reading the Address:

- Look for Willard's numerous reassurances that the education she is recommending for young women would not equal the education received by young men. Like other earlier advocates for women's education, Willard fought for schooling that would be specially suited to the female character and duties. She firmly believed that women had an important role in the domestic sphere and were not suited for professional careers.

- She argues for a better education for women so that they could become better mothers. In fact, she states that the well-being of the nation depends on educated mothers.

- Notice Willard's attack on the substandard female academies that were operating without properly educated and trained teachers.

An Address to the Public Proposing a Plan for Improving Female Education

THE object of this Address, is to convince the public, that a reform, with respect to female education, is necessary; that it cannot be effected by individual exertion, but that it requires the aid of the legislature: and further, by [showing] the justice, the policy, and the **magnanimity** of such an undertaking, to persuade that body, to endow a seminary for females, as the **commencement** of such reformation.

The idea of a college for males, will naturally be associated with that of a seminary, instituted and endowed by the public; and the absurdity of sending ladies to college, may, at first thought, strike every one, to whom this subject shall be proposed. I therefore **hasten** to observe, that the seminary here recommended, will be as different from those **appropriated** to the other sex, as the female character and duties are from the male.—The business of the **husbandman** is not to waste his endeavours, in seeking to make his orchard attain the strength and majesty of his forest, but to rear each, to the perfection of its nature.

That the improvement of female education will be considered by our **enlightened** citizens as a subject of importance, the **liberality** with which they part with their property to educate their daughters, is a sufficient evidence; and why should they not, when assembled in the legislature, act in concert to effect a noble object, which, though dear to them individually, cannot be accomplished by their unconnected exertions.

Magnanimity: Nobleness.
Commencement: The beginning.
Hasten: To urge.
Appropriated: Set aside for a particular purpose.
Husbandman: Farmer.
Enlightened: Informed or learned.
Liberality: Generosity.

Shannon Faulkner and the Citadel

While education was the first area where women began to achieve some measure of equality in the United States, the struggle for equal access to institutions of higher learning continues today. In 1994 a young woman named Shannon Faulkner applied to and was accepted for admission to the Citadel, an all-male military college in Charleston, South Carolina. On her application, she deliberately refrained from answering questions that would have revealed her gender, and she did not submit a photograph of herself to the admissions office. Faulkner was accepted to the school, but when Citadel officials discovered she was a woman, her acceptance was revoked. This action resulted in a lawsuit claiming sex discrimination, the denial of Faulkner's civil rights, and the denial of equal protection under the law (a breach of the Fourteenth Amendment). Faulkner was eventually allowed to enroll in classes in the fall of 1995 while the lawsuit was pending. Unfortunately, she dropped out of the Citadel shortly thereafter, unable to withstand the stress of the experience. The entire incident only deepened the debate about opening the school to women.

*If the improvement of the American female character, and that alone, could be effected by public liberality, employed in giving better means of instruction; such improvement of one half of society, and that half, which **barbarous***

Barbarous: Uncultured.

and **despotic** nations have ever degraded, would of itself be an object, worthy of the most liberal government on earth; but if the female character be raised, it must inevitably raise that of the other sex: and thus does the plan proposed, offer, as the object of legislative **bounty,** to elevate the whole character of the community.

As evidence, that this statement does not exaggerate the female influence in society, our sex need but be considered, in the single relation of mothers. In this character, we have the charge of the whole mass of individuals, who are to compose the succeeding generation; during that period of youth, when the **pliant** mind takes any direction, to which it is steadily guided by a forming hand. How important a power is given by this **charge!** yet, little do too many of my sex know how, either to appreciate or improve it. Unprovided with the means of acquiring that knowledge, which flows liberally to the other sex—having our time of education devoted to **frivolous** acquirements, how should we understand the nature of the mind, so as to be aware of the importance of those early impressions, which we make upon the minds of our children?—or how should we be able to form enlarged and correct views, either of the character, to which we ought to mould them, or of the means most proper to form them aright?

Considered in this point of view, were the interests of male education alone to be consulted, that of females becomes of sufficient importance to engage the public attention. Would we rear the human plant to its perfection, we must first fertilize the soil which produces it. If it acquire its first bent and texture upon a **barren** plain, it will avail comparatively little, should it be afterwards transplanted to a garden....

Thus the writer has endeavored to point out ... that the great cause of these defects consists in a state of things, in which legislatures, undervaluing the importance of women in society, neglect to provide for their education, and suffer it to become the sport of adventurers for fortune, who may be both ignorant and **vicious.**

Despotic: Exercising power abusively.
Bounty: A reward.
Pliant: Easily influenced.
Charge: Responsibility.
Frivolous: Lacking importance.
Barren: Unfruitful.
Vicious: Wicked.

24   E. Willard

It is the duty of a government, to do all in its power to promote the present and future prosperity of the nation, over which it is placed. This prosperity will depend on the character of its citizens. The characters of these will be formed by their mothers; and it is through the mothers, that the government can control the characters of its future citizens, to form them such as will ensure their country's prosperity.... It is the duty of our present legislators to begin now, to form the characters of the next generation, by controling that of the females, who are to be their mothers, while it is yet with them a season of improvement....

The writer has now given a sketch of her plan ... to organize a system of female education, which shall posses the permanency, uniformity of operation, and respectability of our male institutions; and yet differ from them, so as to be adapted, to that difference of character, and duties, to which early instruction should form the softer sex....

*In calling on my patriotic countrymen, to effect so noble an object, the consideration of national glory, should not be overlooked.... Where is that wise and heroic country, which has considered, that our rights are sacred, though we cannot defend them? that tho' a weaker, we are an essential part of the body politic, whose corruption or improvement must affect the whole? and which, having thus considered, has sought to give us by education, that rank in the scale of being, to which our importance entitles us? History shows not that country. It shows many, whose legislatures have sought to improve their various vegetable productions, and their breeds of useful brutes; but none, whose public councils have made it an object of their deliberations, to improve the character of their women. Yet though history lifts not her finger to such an one, **anticipation** does. She points to a nation, which, having thrown off the shackles of authority and precedent, shrinks not from schemes of improvement, because other nations have never attempted them; but which, in its pride of independence, would rather lead than follow, in the march of human improve-*

Anticipation: Looking forward to.

*ment: a nation, wise and magnanimous to plan, enterprising to undertake, and rich in resources to execute. Does not every American **exult** hat this country is his own? And who knows how great and good a race of men, may yet arise from the forming hand of mothers, enlightened by the bounty of that beloved country,—to defend her liberties,—to plan her future improvement,—and to raise her to **unparalleled** glory? (Willard, pp. 4-6, 17, 25, 43, 59)*

What happened next...

While the members of the New York state legislature granted a charter for a female academy in the town of Waterbury, they rejected Willard's request for funding. She then used her own money to publish her plan and began campaigning in Troy, a prosperous town located across the Hudson River from Albany. Eventually the Town Council of Troy voted to raise $4,000 for a building by a special tax, and Willard herself secured additional private funds to cover the expenses of staff members' salaries and maintenance costs. The Troy Female Seminary opened its doors in 1821, becoming the first endowed institution of higher education for females. Over 12,000 women attended the seminary between 1821 and 1872, with many graduates going on to form their own schools. Operated by the Willard family for three generations, today the seminary is known as the Emma Willard School.

Did you know...

- Forbidden from observing the teaching practices used at male schools, Willard devised her own methods for teaching solid geometry by carving cones and pyramids out of turnips and potatoes.

- During the 1830s mothers visiting the Troy Female Seminary were shocked to see a pupil drawing a picture of a heart with arteries and veins. To avoid further controversy, Willard

Exult: Glory.
Unparalleled: Having no match or equal.

Emma Willard

Emma Willard (1787-1870) was born in Berlin, Connecticut, as one of seventeen children. Educated by her father, a bookish Yankee farmer and Revolutionary War captain, she studied and taught at district schools before attending a local academy for a short period of time. While married to a physician and living in Middlebury, Vermont, Willard became a principal of a girls' academy in 1807. Seven years later she opened her own boarding school. Her successes and experiences there led her to develop her plan for women's education in 1819. After founding the Troy Female Seminary in 1821, Willard traveled across the country and lectured extensively in support of universal public education.

pasted heavy paper over any textbook pages containing illustrations of the human body.

- Some historians consider Willard to be the first female lobbyist. (A lobbyist tries to influence public officials to pass specific legislation.)

- Elizabeth Cady Stanton, a famous supporter of women's rights during the second half of the nineteenth century, graduated from the Troy Female Seminary in 1832.

For Further Reading

Goodsell, Willystine. *Pioneers of Women's Education in the United States*. Originally published in 1931. Reprinted. New York: AMS Press, 1970.

Lutz, Alma. *Emma Willard, Daughter of Democracy.* Boston: Beacon Press, 1964.

Willard, Emma. *Mrs. Willard's Plan of Female Education.* 2nd ed. Middlebury, Vermont: Copeland, 1819.

A Treatise on Domestic Economy

Written by Catherine Beecher, 1841
Revised edition published in 1848

A merican educator and writer Catherine Beecher and other early teachers, including Emma Willard, were critical of the typical female seminaries scattered across the United States during the early 1800s. These schools were often run by poorly trained teachers and did not offer young women much opportunity for high quality instruction. Beecher founded the Hartford Female Seminary in 1823 and later wrote a fund-raising pamphlet entitled *Suggestions Respecting Improvements in Education.* In the booklet Beecher urges educators to train young women in domestic science as well as the profession of teaching.

In addition to being an educator, Beecher was a prominent leader in a conservative movement that emphasized a woman's role in the domestic sphere of American culture. Though staunchly independent, she believed that a woman's proper place was in the home, where she could exert a profound, positive influence as a wife and mother. Beecher opposed women's involvement in the antislavery and women's rights movements; she felt that political activity clashed with a woman's

natural domestic responsibilities. In 1837 she attacked popular abolitionist Angelina Grimké in *An Essay on Slavery and Abolitionism with Reference to the Duty of American Females.* Beecher criticized any activity that "throws women into the attitude of a combatant, either for herself or others" because such endeavors lay outside women's "appropriate sphere."

In 1841 Beecher published her major work, *A Treatise on Domestic Economy,* which examines many aspects of home life. One of the most popular books of her time, *A Treatise* went through 15 editions. In the book, Beecher provides students and homemakers with practical advice concerning cooking, family health, infant care, and many other topics. She collaborated with her sister, author Harriet Beecher Stowe, on one of the most popular revisions of *A Treatise—The American Woman's Home*—which was published in 1869.

Catherine Beecher's sister Harriet Beecher Stowe wrote the classic novel Uncle Tom's Cabin.

Things to Remember While Reading
A Treatise on Domestic Economy:
- Notice Beecher's belief that a competent homemaker required an extensive period of training, one that was as technical and rigorous as legal or medical training. In fact, *A Treatise* contains over 350 pages of detailed instructions about everything from proper room ventilation to household budgets.

- Beecher intended her instructional book to serve as both a textbook to young female students and an advice manual for homemakers.

- In the nineteenth century daughters of wealthy families were frequently sent away to study frivolous, or useless, subjects—a practice Beecher opposed.

- Beecher's last comment in the preface states that part of the proceeds from the sale of her book would help fund the costs of training and relocating teachers for service in the expanding U.S. territories, where there was a shortage of schools.

A Treatise on Domestic Economy

PREFACE TO THE THIRD EDITION

*The author of this work was led to attempt it, by discovering, in her extensive travels, the **deplorable** sufferings of multitudes of young wives and mothers, from the combined influence of poor health, poor domestics, and a defective domestic education....*

*The writer became early convinced that this evil results mainly from the fact, that young girls, especially in the more wealthy classes, are not trained for their profession. In early life, they go through a course of school training which results in great **debility** of **constitution,** while, at the same time, their physical and domestic education is almost **wholly** neglected. Thus they enter on their most **arduous** and sacred duties so inexperienced and uninformed, and with so little muscular and nervous strength, that probably there is not one chance in ten, that young women of the present day, will pass through the first years of married life without such **prostration** of health and spirits as makes life a burden to themselves, and, it is to be feared, such as seriously interrupts the confidence and happiness of married life.*

The measure which, more than any other, would tend to remedy this evil, would be to place domestic economy *on an equality with the other sciences in female schools. This should be done because it* can *be properly and systematically taught (*not *practically, but as a science), as much so as political economy or moral science, or any other branch of study; because it embraces knowledge, which will be needed by young women at all times and in all places; because this science can never be properly taught until it is made a branch of study; and because this method will secure a dignity and importance in the estimation of young girls, which can never be accorded while they perceive their teachers and parents prac-*

Deplorable: Wretched; awful.

Debility: Weakened state.

Constitution: Physical structure of an individual's body.

Wholly: Completely.

Arduous: Difficult.

Prostration: Reduced to exhaustion.

tically attaching more value to every other department of science than this. When young ladies are taught the construction of their own bodies, and all the causes in domestic life which tend to weaken the constitution; when they are taught rightly to appreciate and learn the most convenient and economical modes of performing all family duties, and of employing time and money; and when they perceive the true estimate accorded to these things by teachers and friends, the grand cause of this evil will be removed. Women will be trained to secure, as of first importance, a strong and healthy constitution, and all those rules of thrift and economy that will make domestic duty easy and pleasant.

To promote this object, the writer prepared this volume as a text-book for female schools. It has been examined by the Massachusetts Board of Education, and been deemed worthy by them to be admitted as part of the Massachusetts School Library.

It has also been adopted as a text-book in some of our largest and most popular female schools, both at the East and West.

The following, from the pen of Mr. George B. Emmerson, one of the most popular and successful teachers in our country, who has introduced this work as a text-book in his own school, will exhibit the opinion of one who has formed his judgment from experience in the use of the work:

It may be objected that such things cannot be taught by books. Why not? Why may not the structure of the human body, and the laws of health **deduced** therefrom, be as well taught as the laws of natural philosophy? Why are not the application of these laws to the management of infants and young children as important to a woman as the application of the rules of arithmetic to the extraction of the **cube root?** Why may not the properties of the atmosphere be explained, in reference to the proper ventilation of rooms, or exercise in the open

Deduced: *Reasoned.*

Cube root: *A mathematical concept. (A number multiplied by itself three times is said to be cubed. The number 3 is the cube root of 27 because 3 cubed is 27.)*

Beecher

Catherine Beecher

Catherine Beecher (1800-1878), the oldest of eight children in an extremely influential family, was born in East Hampton, on Long Island, New York. She was the daughter of Lyman Beecher, a famous minister and temperance leader (one who advocated abstinence from alcohol). Harriet Beecher Stowe, author of the classic *Uncle Tom's Cabin*, was her sister, and the minister Henry Ward Beecher was her brother. In addition to being a leading educator, Catherine Beecher was a famous writer. In fact, according to one biographer, Beecher wrote so many successful books that she was probably able to support herself and her causes with the money she earned from royalties.

air, as properly as to the burning of steel or sodium? Why is not the human skeleton as curious and interesting as the air-pump; and the action of the brain, as the action of a steam-engine?... For ourselves, we have always found children, especially girls, peculiarly ready to listen to what they saw would prepare them for future duties. The truth, that education should be a preparation for actual, real life, has the greatest force with children. The constantly-recurring inquiry, 'What will be the use of this study?' is always satisfied by showing, that it will prepare for any duty, relation, or office which, in the natural course of things, will be likely to come.

We think this book extremely well suited to be used as a text-book in schools for young ladies, and many chapters are well adapted for a reading book for children of both sexes.

To this the writer would add the testimony of a lady who has used this work with several classes of young girls and young ladies. She remarked that she had never known a school-book that awakened more interest, and that some young girls would learn a lesson in this when they would study nothing else....

*Although the writer was trained to the care of children, and to perform all branches of domestic duty, by some of the best housekeepers, much in these pages is offered, not as the result of her own experience, but as what has obtained the approbation of some of the most **judicious** mothers and housekeepers in the nation. The articles on Physiology and Hygiene, and those on horticulture, were derived from standard works on these subjects, and are sanctioned by the highest authorities....*

*The copyright interest in these two works is held by a board of gentlemen appointed for the purpose, who, after paying a moderate **compensation** to the author for the time and labour spent in preparing these works, will employ all the remainder paid over by the publishers, to aid in educating and locating such female teachers as wish to be employed in those portions of our country, which are most destitute of schools. (Beecher, pp. 3-9)*

What happened next...

Beecher spent her life working for her two favorite causes: advancing the domestic role of women and improving the growing field of education. She worked very hard to increase aware-

Judicious: Having good judgment.
Compensation: Monetary payment or salary.

ness of the shortage of teachers in America's newly settled western regions. In 1845 Beecher published *The Duty of American Women to Their Country,* which urged women to become teachers for the nation's two million unschooled children. Through her service on the Board of National Popular Education, she helped select, train, and place over five hundred New England schoolteachers in 1847. She went on to organize the American Women's Educational Association, which helped establish female colleges in the West where girls could be trained as both teachers and homemakers. One of these schools, Milwaukee-Downer College, still exists today.

Did you know...

- When Beecher's fiance tragically died at sea, her minister-father viewed this death as a sign from God indicating that her life would be different from that of other women.

- Catherine Beecher's sister, Harriet Beecher Stowe, published *Uncle Tom's Cabin* in 1851. While Catherine was much more famous than Harriet during their era, today the opposite is true.

- Beecher's grandniece, Charlotte Perkins Gilman, contributed to the public debate regarding women's need for better employment opportunities with her book *Women and Economics,* published in 1898.

For Further Reading

Beecher, Catherine E. *A Treatise on Domestic Economy, for the Use of Young Ladies at Home, and at School.* Rev ed. New York: Harper & Brothers, 1848.

Goodsell, Willystine. *Pioneers of Women's Education in the United States.* Originally published in 1931. Reprinted. New York: AMS Press, 1970.

Sklar, Kathryn Kish. *Catherine Beecher: A Study in Domesticity.* New York: W. W. Norton, 1976.

Abolition

No struggle in American history exerted a more profound effect on the course of women's rights than the abolition (or antislavery) movement. The moral, social, and economic questions about the institution of slavery created a deep division in pre-Civil War America.

Through their involvement with the abolitionist cause, women became experienced activists familiar with the potential of organized reform efforts. When they initially immersed themselves in antislavery efforts in the 1830s, American women formed their own groups and met separately from men. As the movement accelerated and grew, individual women emerged as powerful public speakers and became influential leaders. Among them were **Lucretia Mott**, sisters Angelina and **Sarah Grimké**, and **Sojourner Truth**.

The Grimké sisters toured the Northeast in the 1830s speaking out against the practice of slavery and the "lesser question" of women's rights. Their talks drew the attention of church leaders, who in a public letter condemned their lectures. Sarah

Grimké agreed to stop speaking about women's issues and instead began publishing essays promoting a woman's right to participate in public affairs. The pastoral letter that denounced the Grimkés was itself the target of satire by abolitionist **Maria Weston Chapman**. Chapman attacked the clergymen in her poem "The Times That Try Men's Souls," which appeared in the antislavery paper *The Liberator* in 1837.

Quaker abolitionist Lucretia Mott helped form the American Anti-Slavery Society in 1833 and was later elected to serve as a delegate to the World Anti-Slavery Convention in London. At the London convention, however, Mott and other female delegates were not permitted to sit with the male delegates or participate fully in the proceedings.

Mott's outrage over the treatment she received at the World Anti-Slavery Convention helped inspire **Elizabeth Cady Stanton** to action. Stanton and Mott met for the first time in London and developed a lifelong mutual devotion to the cause of promoting women's rights. In 1848 they organized the first women's rights convention in Seneca Falls, New York. Stanton used the convention to publicize her Declaration of Sentiments, which in many regards outlined the goals for the women's movement in America.

Newspaper publisher, abolitionist, and former slave **Frederick Douglass** wholeheartedly endorsed the Seneca Falls convention and wrote a glowing report of the unprecedented event in his abolitionist newspaper *The North Star*. As news of the Seneca Falls convention spread throughout the Northeast, a second convention was held in Rochester. A national debate soon grew over the issue of women's rights.

An ex-slave and active supporter of women's rights, Sojourner Truth traveled throughout the United States in the 1850s preaching liberty for all, regardless of race or gender. Her convictions and honesty made her a moving public speaker. Truth is probably best remembered for her stirring speech "Ain't I a Woman?" **Anna E. Dickinson** was another highly gifted abolitionist speaker of the Civil War era. In fact, Dickinson helped convert so many resistant northerners to the Republican cause of abolition that she received an invitation to address Congress and President Abraham Lincoln in 1864.

Female abolitionists helped make slavery a political issue on a national scale, mainly through their work organizing large petition drives. Men greatly outnumbered female abolitionists, yet women made more significant contributions in terms of petitioning, which required volunteers to circulate forms door to door. The antislavery newspaper *The Liberator* estimated that women sent twice as many petitions to Congress as did men. In fact, the House of Representatives passed "gag" resolutions to stop discussion of the numerous petitions, which in effect prevented discussion of the slavery issue.

With the ratification of the **Thirteenth Amendment** to the Constitution on December 18, 1865, slavery came to an end in the United States. Even after this historic victory, though, many abolitionists continued their efforts to secure full equality for both ex-slaves and women, especially in the area of voting rights. A significant number of women who began their public careers as abolitionists later became leaders in the women's rights movement.

Letters on the Equality of the Sexes and the Condition of Woman

Written by Sarah Moore Grimké
Published as a pamphlet, 1838

Antislavery activities became increasing popular during the 1830s. As more women became involved in the process, they formed their own societies. The hard work of female abolitionists did not go unnoticed by their male counterparts. In 1836 the all-male American Anti-Slavery Society hired its first female abolition agents—two sisters named Angelina and Sarah Grimké—to give public speeches. Daughters of a wealthy, slaveholding family in South Carolina, the Grimkés grew up witnessing the hardships of slavery firsthand.

The sisters originally intended to speak to all-female groups in private homes. Their popularity, however, led them to larger spaces such as churches, where it was impossible to forbid men from attending. The Grimkés urged their audiences to realize that men and women have equal responsibility regarding moral issues. But controversy soon began to surround the duo, since their public speaking about political issues was considered "promiscuous" or unladylike. Thereafter, clergymen refused to read announcements of the Grimké lectures and denied them the use of their churches.

The harshest protest occurred in 1837 in the "Pastoral Letter of the General Association of Congregational Ministers of Massachusetts." The letter, which was read from church pulpits and widely circulated, accused the sisters of unwomanly and un-Christian behavior. Male abolitionist leaders advised the sisters to lecture only about slavery and not to discuss the "lesser questions" of women's rights. While the Grimké sisters agreed to limit their public speeches to slavery, they also began to publish essays concerned with the "woman question."

Sarah Grimké's most famous work consists of letters written to her friend, Mary S. Parker, president of the Boston Female Anti-Slavery Society. These letters reflect the first serious discussion of women's rights by an American woman.

Sarah Grimké's sister Angelina was also a fiery orator.

Things to Remember While Reading *Letters:*

* Grimké based her argument for the equality between the sexes on the Bible, the very source her critics used in their attacks against her.

* She accuses the male church leaders of interpreting the Bible to suit their wishes and further states that there is no biblical justification for an inferior position for women.

* Grimké believed that God does not distinguish between men and women and that members of both sexes are moral and intelligent beings.

* Her writings support women's active role in all moral pursuits.

Letters on the Equality of the Sexes and the Condition of Woman

Haverhill, 7th Mo. 1837

Dear Friend,

When I last addressed thee, I had not seen the Pastoral Letter of the General Association [of Congregational Ministers of Massachusetts]. It has since fallen into my hands, and I must digress from my intention of exhibiting the condition of women in different parts of the world, in order to make some remarks on this extraordinary document....

*[The letter] says, "We invite your attention to the dangers which at present seem to threaten the FEMALE CHARACTER with wide-spread and permanent injury." I rejoice that they have called the attention of my sex to this subject, because I believe if woman investigates it, she will soon discover that danger is impending, though from a totally different source from that which the Association apprehends,—danger from those who, having long held the reins of **usurped** authority, are unwilling to permit us to fill that sphere which God created us to move in, and who have entered into league to crush the immortal mind of woman. I rejoice, because I am persuaded that the rights of woman, like the rights of slaves, need only be examined to be understood and asserted, even by some of those, who are now endeavoring to smother the irrepressible desire for mental and spiritual freedom which glows in the breast of many, who hardly dare to speak their sentiments.*

*"The appropriate duties and influence of women are clearly stated in the New Testament. Those duties are **unobtrusive** and private, but the sources of mighty power. When the mild, dependent, softening influence of woman upon the sternness of man's opinions is fully exercised, society feels the*

Usurped: *Seized power or authority wrongfully.*
Unobtrusive: *Not loud or showy.*

Grimké

effects of it in a thousand ways." No one can desire more earnestly than I do, that woman may move exactly in the sphere which her Creator has assigned her; and I believe her having been displaced from that sphere has introduced confusion into the world. It is, therefore, of vast importance to herself and to all the rational creation, that she should ascertain what are her duties and her privileges as a responsible and immortal being. The New Testament has been referred to, and I am willing to abide by its decisions, but must enter my protest against the false translation of some passages by the MEN who did that work, and against the perverted interpretation by the MEN who undertook to write commentaries thereon. I am inclined to think, when we are admitted to the honor of studying Greek and Hebrew, we shall produce some various readings of the Bible a little different from those we now have.

The Lord Jesus defines the duties of his followers in his Sermon on the Mount. He lays down grand principles by which they should be governed, without any reference to sex or condition.—"Ye are the light of the world. A city that is set on a hill cannot be hid. Neither do men light a candle and put it under a bushel, but on a candlestick, and it giveth light unto all that are in the house. Let your light so shine before men, that they may see your good works, and glorify your Father which is in Heaven" [Matt. 5:14-16]. I follow him through all his **precepts,** and find him giving the same directions to women as to men, never even referring to the distinction now so strenuously insisted upon between masculine and feminine virtues: this is one of the anti-christian "traditions of men" which are taught instead of the "commandments of God." Men and women were CREATED EQUAL; they are both moral and accountable beings, and whatever is right for man to do, is right for woman.

But the influence of woman, says the Association, is to be private and unobtrusive; her light is not to shine before man like that of her **brethren;** but she is passively to let the lords of the creation, as they call themselves, put the bushel over it, lest

Precepts: *Principles used to guide action.*
Brethren: *Brothers.*

"The Times That Try Men's Souls"

Written by Maria Weston Chapman, 1837

Maria Weston Chapman (1806-1885) was instrumental in spreading information about the abolitionist movement in New England. She organized and later led the Boston Anti-Slavery Society, which was founded in 1832. Together with William Lloyd Garrison—publisher of the abolitionist paper *The Liberator*—Chapman helped solidify support for the controversial Grimké sisters as they lectured throughout New England in 1837. The Grimkés came under harsh attack in the "Pastoral Letter" written by the Council of Congregationalist Ministers of Massachusetts, who charged it was unnatural and un-Christian for women to "assume the place and tone of a man as a public reformer." Chapman wrote and circulated an equally terse satire, or sarcastic poem, in response to the letter. The first stanza of the poem, "The Times That Try Men's Souls," follows:

> Confusion has seized us, and all
>   things go wrong,
> The women have leaped from
>   "their spheres,"
> And, instead of fixed stars, shoot
>   as comets along,
> And are setting the world by the
>   ears!
> In course erratic they're wheeling
>   through space,
> In brainless confusion and mean-
>   ingless chase.

peradventure it might appear that the world has been benefitted by the rays of her candle. So that her quenched light, according to their judgment, will be of more use than if it were set on the candlestick. "Her influence is the source of mighty power." This has ever been the flattering language of man since he laid aside the whip as a means to keep woman in **subjection.** He spare her body; but the war he has waged against her mind, her heart, and her soul, has been no less destructive to her as a moral being. How monstrous, how anti-christian, is the doctrine that woman is to be dependent on man! Where, in all the sacred Scriptures, is this taught? Alas! she has too well learned the lesson, which MAN has labored to teach her. She has surrendered her dearest RIGHTS, and been satisfied with the

Peradventure: By chance.
Subjection: Forced to submit.

privileges which man has assumed to grant her; she has been amused with the show of power, whilst man has absorbed all the reality into himself. He has adorned the creature whom God gave him as a companion, with **baubles** and **gewgaws,** turned her attention to personal attractions, offered incense to her vanity, and made her the instrument of his selfish gratification, a plaything to please his eye and amuse his hours of leisure. "Rule by obedience and by submission sway," or in other words, study to be a hypocrite, pretend to submit, but gain your point, has been the code of household morality which woman has been taught. The poet has sung, in sickly strains, the loveliness of woman's dependence upon man, and now we find it reechoed by those who profess to teach the religion of the Bible. God says, "Cease ye from man whose breath is in his nostrils, for wherein is he to be accounted of?" Man says, depend upon me. God says, "HE will teach us of his ways." Man says, believe it not, I am to be your teacher. This doctrine of dependence upon man is utterly at variance with the doctrine of the Bible. In that book I find nothing like the softness of woman, nor the sternness of man: both are equally commanded to bring forth the fruits of the Spirit, love, meekness, gentleness, &c.

But we are told, "the power of woman is in her dependence, flowing from a consciousness of that weakness which God has given her for her protection." If physical weakness is alluded to, I cheerfully concede the superiority; if brute force is what my brethren are claiming, I am willing to let them have all the honor they desire; but if they mean to **intimate**, that mental or moral weakness belongs to woman, more than to man, I utterly disclaim the charge. Our powers of mind have been crushed, as far as man could do it, our sense of morality has been impaired by his interpretation of our duties; but no where does God say that he made any distinction between us, as moral and intelligent beings....

The General Association say, that "when woman assumes the place and tone of man as a public reformer, our care and protection of her seem unnecessary; we put ourselves in self-

Baubles: *Trinkets or ornaments such as jewelry.*
Gewgaws: *Flashy or showy things of little value.*
Intimate: *Declare.*

defence against her, and her character becomes unnatural." Here again the unscriptural notion is held up, that there is a distinction between the duties of men and women as moral beings; that what is virtue in man, is vice in woman; and women who dare to obey the command of Jehovah, "Cry aloud, spare not, lift up thy voice like a trumpet, and show my people their **transgression**" [Isa. 58:1], are threatened with having the protection of the brethren withdrawn. If this is all they do, we shall not even know the time when our **chastisement** is inflicted; our trust is in the Lord Jehovah, and in him is everlasting strength. The motto of woman, when she is engaged in the great work of public reformation should be,—"The Lord is my light and my salvation; whom shall I fear? The Lord is the strength of my life; of whom shall I be afraid?" [Ps. 27:1]. She must feel, if she feels rightly, that she is fulfilling one of the important duties laid upon her as an accountable being, and that her character, instead of being "unnatural," is in exact accordance with the will of Him to whom, and to no other, she is responsible for the talents and the gifts confided to her. As to the pretty simile, introduced into the "Pastoral Letter," "If the vine whose strength and beauty is to lean upon the trellis work, and half conceal its clusters, thinks to assume the independence and the overshadowing nature of the elm," &c. I shall only remark that it might well suit the poet's fancy, who sings of sparkling eyes and coral lips, and knights in armor clad; but it seems to me utterly inconsistent with the dignity of a Christian body, to endeavor to draw such an anti-scriptural distinction between men and women. Ah! how many of my sex feel in the **dominion**, thus unrighteously exercised over them, under the gentle **appellation** of protection, that what they have leaned upon has proved a broken reed at best, and oft a spear.

Thine in the bonds of womanhood,

Sarah M. Grimké (Bartlett, pp. 37-41)

Transgression: Violation of a law, command, or duty; a sin.
Chastisement: Punishment.
Dominion: Absolute power.
Appellation: Name.

Sarah Moore Grimké

Sarah Moore Grimké (1792-1873) was born in Charleston, South Carolina, in 1792. The sixth child of a wealthy, slaveholding family, she received her education at home by studying with her brother and secretly thought about becoming a lawyer. Grimké helped raise her younger sister, Angelina, and also taught slaves how to read. Both sisters moved to Philadelphia after converting to the Quaker faith. Sarah never married even though she received two marriage proposals. After the sisters retired from the speaking circuit, they concentrated on the "domestic sphere." Angelina married abolitionist Theodore Weld in 1838 and, together with Sarah, they settled in Fort Lee, New Jersey.

What happened next...

The Grimkés ended their careers as public speakers in 1838. Their defense of women's rights led to the 1839 decision of the American Anti-Slavery Society to allow women as full members who could hold office within the organization and serve as public lecturers.

The sisters' few years of abolitionist work highlight the major impact that female abolition societies had on the emerging question of women's rights. The female abolitionists and their organizations were forerunners of the suffrage movement, which sought women's right to vote. More than previous benevolent or reform work, such as the female seminary movement, abolitionism engaged women in public debate and raised questions about their own status in society. Women involved in the fight against slavery became familiar with issues of human rights and limits on freedom—principles that applied to the condition of women as well as to slaves.

Did you know...

- Sarah and Angelina Grimké were actually the first professional women reformers of any American organization.

- With the exception of female Quaker ministers, it was regarded as highly improper in the early 1800s for women to speak to or meet with men outside of their home.

- Sarah Grimké's *Letters* was the first serious work by an American woman about the "woman question." It appeared ten years before the Seneca Falls Convention and seven years before Margaret Fuller's *Woman in the Nineteenth Century.*

For Further Reading

Bartlett, Elizabeth Ann, ed. *Sarah Grimké: Letters on the Equality of the Sexes and Other Essays.* New Haven, Connecticut: Yale University Press, 1988.

Flexner, Eleanor. *Century of Struggle: The Woman's Rights Movement in the United States.* Revised edition. Cambridge, Massachusetts: Belknap/Harvard University Press, 1975.

Lerner, Gerder. *The Grimké Sisters from South Carolina: Pioneers for Women's Rights and Abolition.* New York: Schocken Books, 1967.

Rappoport, Doreen, ed. *American Women: Their Lives in Their Words.* New York: HarperCollins, 1990.

Diary Entries

Written by Lucretia Mott
World Anti-Slavery Convention
London, England
May-June 1840

Lucretia Mott was a deeply religious woman who became an official minister of the Society of Friends (a Christian sect that promotes justice, peace, and simplicity in living) in 1821, when she was 28 years old. Around that time Mott and other Quakers—as members of the Society of Friends are called—began to actively protest slavery by boycotting, or not buying, products made or grown in the South. They used substitutes for cotton, sugar, rice, and other common goods needed for everyday life. By 1829 Mott's antislavery activities also included visiting black churches to give sermons—a practice considered highly improper by the white establishment.

Working closely with abolitionist William Lloyd Garrison and others, Mott helped found the American Anti-Slavery Society in 1833. One of its more radical members, Mott believed in immediate freedom for slaves as opposed to the more conservative idea of granting freedom gradually. When the American Anti-Slavery Society no longer permitted women members, she

Mott and her husband James (bottom row, far right) pose with members of the Pennsylvania Anti-Slavery Society in 1839.

helped start Philadelphia's Women Society and served as its president for many years.

Mott and others who lectured frequently against slavery put themselves at great risk of physical harm. In 1838 protesters burned Pennsylvania Hall in Philadelphia after a speech by abolitionist Maria Weston Chapman. Mott courageously helped lead women out of the burning building and never once considered ending her work as a public speaker.

In 1840, when Mott was 47 years old, she was elected to serve as an official delegate from the American Anti-Slavery Society to the World Anti-Slavery Convention, held that year in London. Unfortunately, after Mott and her husband had already set sail for England, their British hosts decided not to allow women to attend the convention. In the week leading up to the meeting, Mott attempted to persuade British Friends to reverse their decision. Although in the end she lost her battle—she and the other women had to sit in a roped-off section of the auditorium—Mott won in many other regards. She met many interesting people in London, including Elizabeth Cady Stanton, the trailblazing young wife of Henry B. Stanton, a leading American abolitionist.

Mott brought along a small black diary with her when she and her husband set off on May 7, 1840, aboard the steamer ship *Roscoe*. The Motts traveled with the other members of the Pennsylvania delegation, several young women among them, including Sarah Pugh. As they were all to discover, British abolitionists, both male and female, were not willing to include women in the convention proceedings—even if they were official delegates sent from the United States.

Things to Remember While Reading the Diary Entries:

- Mott used numbers instead of names for the days of the week. For example, Sunday is number 1, Monday is number 2, etc.

- Notice her sharp attack against Nathaniel Colver, a member of the New Organization, a recently formed American antislavery group that did not look kindly on women's involvement.

- Mott notes her growing friendship with Elizabeth Cady Stanton.

- Mott argues that the British and Foreign Anti-Slavery Society actually based its work on a doctrine, or philosophy, recommended by a woman. British Friend Elizabeth Heyrick was the first to suggest that abolitionists should focus on "immediate emancipation"—freedom for the slaves right away rather than gradually.

Diary Entries

7th Day [June] 6th. Joseph Sturge breakfasted with us— begged submission of us to the London Committee—read a letter from [British antislavery pioneer] Thomas Clarkson on the subject—acknowledged he had received letters from Amer-

ica on the same subject—made great **professions**—invited us to tea at the Anti-Slavery rooms with such of the Delegates as had arrived. We endeavored to [show] him the inconsistency of excluding Women Delegates—but soon found he had pre-judged & made up his mind to act with our New Organization [the American and Foreign Anti-Slavery Society]; therefore all reasoning was lost upon him, and our appeals made in vain.... Evening visit to the Anti-Slavery rooms pleasant & interesting— This is a common practice in England. When committees meet they have tea & invite company to join them, after which they appoint a chairman & make the conversation general. William D. Crewdson was chairman—addressed his friends by the title of "Mr."—Conversation on the **expediency** of continuing such conventions—[I] enquired if they, as well as all our [recent?] efforts were based on the duty of "immediate emancipation." On being answered affirmatively, gave them to understand that this originating with E[lizabeth] Heyrick—a woman, when the convention should be held in America, we should not contem-plate the exclusion of Women. Many spoke kindly to us, some responded "hear, hear"! all were pleasant. Elizabeth Pease the only female present beside ourselves—about 25 men....

3rd day. [June] 9th.... William Ball came with official information that Women were to be rejected. Asked Colver & Galusha if they had heard that similar course was to be pur-sued toward the new organization—alarmed them. Much talk till after 12 o'clock....

4th day [June]. 10th. Joseph Sturge & Scales called to endeavor to reconcile us to our fate—called a meeting of women to protest.... Tea again at Anti-Slavery rooms.... [Topic of] **free produce** introduced, called on me to speak—replied that we had been asked why we could not get the gentlemen to say for us all we wished, so now I would request Henry Grew or [my husband] James Mott to speak for me—insisted on my going on—gave some **rubs** on our proposed exclu-sion—cries of hear!, hear!,—offended Colver—told me I should have been **called to order** if I had not been a woman....

Professions: Declarations or strong statements.
Expediency: Usefulness.
Free produce: The boycotting of goods made in the South as a form of protest.
Rubs: Annoying reminders.
Call to order: Formal request to follow the rules of the meeting.

5th day [June] 11th.... Met again about our exclusion—William Boultbee wished to have our decision—talked much with him, liked him—agreed on the following Protest:

> *The American Women Delegates from Pennsylvania to the World's Convention would present to the Committee of the British & Foreign Anti-Slavery Society their grateful acknowledgments for the kind attentions received by them since their arrival in London. But while as individuals they return thanks for these favors, as delegates from the bodies appointing them, they deeply regret to learn by a series of resolutions passed at a Meeting of your Committee ... that it is contemplated to exclude women from a seat in the convention, as co-equals in the advocacy of Universal Liberty. The Delegates will duly communicate to their constituents, the intimation which these resolutions convey: in the mean time they stand prepared to co-operate to any extent, and in any form, consistent with their instructions, in promoting the just objects of the Convention, to whom it is presumed will belong the power of determining the validity of any claim to a seat in that body.*

On behalf of the Delegates

very respectfully

Sarah Pugh

*6 Mo. 11th. 40.... Evening. Several sent to us to persuade us not to offer ourselves to the Convention—Colver rather bold in his suggestions—answered & of course offended him. W. Morgan & Scales informed us "it wasn't designed as a World Convention—that was a mere **Poetical license**," & that all power would rest with the "London Committee of Arrangements." Prescod of Jamaica (colored) thought it would lower the dignity of the Convention and bring ridicule on the whole thing if ladies were admitted—he was told that similar reasons were urged in Pennsylvania for the exclusion of colored people from our meetings—but had we yielded on such flim-*

Poetical license: *An interpretation that suits one's own needs.*

Lucretia Coffin Mott

Born in Nantucket, Massachusetts, Lucretia Mott (1793-1880) frequently helped her mother run their island household while her father was away on long voyages at sea. Raised as a Quaker, she was schooled in Poughkeepsie, New York, and moved to Philadelphia in 1809. She married James Mott in 1811 and became a Quaker minister ten years later.

Mott was a popular speaker on the topic of abolition and women's rights. Following the Civil War she was named president of the American Equal Rights Association and fought valiantly for black voting rights. She remained active in many causes, including the struggle for world peace, until her death at age 87.

sy arguments, we might as well have abandoned our enterprise. Colver thought Women constitutionally unfit for public or business meetings—he was told that the colored man too was said to be constitutionally *unfit to mingle with the white man.* He left the room angry.

6th day 6 Mo. 12th. The World's Convention—alias the "Conference of the British and Foreign Anti-Slavery Society," with such guests as they chose to invite, assembled. We were kindly admitted behind the **bar**—politely conducted to our seats and introduced to many, whom we had not before met.... Meeting opened in a dignified manner—silence observed.... S. Prescod was warned that his conduct would be watched & he must be on his guard not to compromise "the dignity of the convention." He was the first however to bring ridicule on

Bar: Railing.

himself & to throw the meeting into confusion by improper mention of the "Goddess Delegates."... William Ashurst pointed them to the inconsistency of calling a "World's Convention" to abolish Slavery—and at its threshold depriving half the world their liberty....

6th day [June] 19th.... J. Sturge came to us—doubted whether the ladies would have a meeting—they feared other subjects would be introduced and he partook of the fear. Some were then invited to meet us at our lodgings—much disappointed to find so little independent action on the part of women. Called a Meeting of the Delegates in the evening—so that such as were dissatisfied might prepare a protest....

7th day [June] 20th.... Elizabeth Stanton gaining daily in our affections—hope she may be a blessing to her H.B.S....

3rd day [June] 23rd. Last day of the Convention—some excitement about the protest—Scoble & others begged it might be presented to the committee instead of the Meeting.... Protest offered. Colver boldly & impudently moved that it be laid on the table—afterward made a crying, farewell speech, completely disgusted with him.... Scales made excellent closing remarks that altho' on some subjects they had conflicting sentiments— dividing them "distinct as the billows"—yet he believed there was unity enough in our common cause to make us again "one as the Sea." And so the Convention closed! (Tolles, pp. 22-43)

What happened next...

The events at the World Convention in London forged a lasting friendship between Mott and Stanton. In 1848 they helped organize the first women's rights convention in Seneca Falls, New York. The Declaration of Sentiments agreed upon by this convention laid the framework for the women's rights movement from 1848 to 1919.

Throughout her life Mott remained active in both the abolitionist and women's rights movements. She led many of the early women's rights conventions, frequently presiding as chair or president. When the Civil War erupted, Mott and many of her Quaker friends were torn between their desire to end slavery and their antiwar beliefs (or pacifism). Mott later became vice-president of the Pennsylvania Peace Society and helped raise money for the newly freed slaves.

Did you know...

- Mott wrote a book, *Discourse on Women,* in 1850, discussing the limitations placed on women at that time.

- In 1864 Mott, along with other Quakers, founded Pennsylvania's Swarthmore College.

- She and her husband, James, enjoyed an unusually modern marriage, with James willing to support her causes no matter how radical or disruptive. The couple was married for 57 years.

- Mott usually wore the traditional clothing of a Quaker woman —a white kerchief across her shoulders, a white cap, and plain bonnet.

For Further Reading

Bacon, Margaret Hope. *Valiant Friend: The Life of Lucretia Mott.* New York: Walker & Co., 1980.

Flexner, Eleanor. *Century of Struggle: The Woman's Rights Movement in the United States.* Revised edition. Cambridge, Massachusetts: Belknap/Harvard University Press, 1975.

Mott, Lucretia. *Slavery and "The Woman Question": Lucretia Mott's Diary of Her Visit to Great Britain to Attend the World's Anti-Slavery Convention of 1840.* Edited by Frederick B. Tolles. London: Friends' Historical Society, 1952.

Declaration of Sentiments

Written and delivered by Elizabeth Cady Stanton
First Women's Rights Convention
Seneca Falls, New York
July 19-20, 1848

In many respects, the 1848 Seneca Falls convention marked the beginning of the political, social, and cultural movement for women's rights in America. Through their involvement with antislavery efforts, many women in pre-Civil War America became experienced activists who recognized the power of organized reform movements. As the antislavery movement accelerated and grew, individual women of the nineteenth century gained skill in public speaking and became influential reform leaders. Among them were American preacher, abolitionist, and former slave Sojourner Truth; feminist, activist, and antislavery organizer Lucretia Mott; and sisters Angelina and Sarah Grimké, the socially enlightened children of South Carolina slaveholders.

While framing their arguments for black equality, female abolitionists—as members of the antislavery movement were called—became increasingly aware of their own inferior status in society. In fact, controversy over the role of women disrupted the 1840 World Anti-Slavery Convention held in London, Eng-

Newspaper Announcement of Woman's Rights Convention

WOMAN'S RIGHTS CONVEN-TION—A Convention to discuss the social, civil, and religious condition and rights of woman, will be held in the Wesleyan Chapel, at Seneca Falls, N.Y., on Wednesday and Thursday the 19th and 20th of July, current; commencing at 10 o'clock A.M. During the first day the meeting will be exclusively for women, who are earnestly invited to attend. The public generally are invited to be present on the second day, when Lucretia Mott, of Philadelphia, and other ladies and gentlemen, will address the convention. (Stanton et al., p. 67)

land. After heated debate, female attendees were forced to listen to the proceedings in a curtained-off section of the auditorium. At the convention, Mott first met Elizabeth Cady Stanton, the wife of leading abolitionist Henry Stanton. Mott, a Quaker minister and an organizer and official delegate of the American Anti-Slavery Society, supported human rights for both women and slaves. Stanton shared this view, as well as a general frustration concerning the treatment of women at the convention. At the close of the proceedings, Mott and Stanton resolved to one day sponsor an assembly dedicated to discussing women's rights.

Over the next eight years, the two women corresponded frequently and shared their ideas. In 1848 Mott invited Stanton to visit her in a nearby town. During her stay, Stanton spoke with her friend and with several other Quaker women about the political and social status of women in the United States. Stanton's views moved her listeners to action. The group decided to call a public meeting to discuss women's rights. They announced the gathering in the July 14th edition of the *Seneca County Courier,* a local newspaper in central New York.

Despite the short notice, over three hundred people (including 40 men) attended the two-day convention, which was held in the Seneca Falls Methodist Church. Mott's husband, James, chaired the meeting. After several other lecturers spoke, Stanton read her Declaration of Sentiments, a document she patterned after the principles in the Declaration of Independence. In her speech, Stanton included a woman's right to vote (also known as "suffrage" or "franchise") among twelve resolutions put forth for discussion and adoption. Fearing that the goal of suffrage would make them look foolish, Mott and several other organizers objected to this bold and revolutionary resolution. But despite the difference of opinion, all of the resolutions—including the suffrage proposal—were unanimously adopted. Approximately one-third of the convention's attendees signed their names to the Declaration of Sentiments.

Things to Remember While Reading the "Declaration of Sentiments:"

- There are numerous similarities between Stanton's speech and the Declaration of Independence.

- In 1848 it was unusual for women to speak in public, testify in court, preach in churches, and work in most professions.

- At the time Stanton gave her speech, it was common for married women to lose basic rights, such as the freedom to own property, control earned wages, and maintain custody over their children if a marriage ended in separation or divorce.

- The ninth of Stanton's twelve resolutions—the one calling for women's suffrage—was considered a very radical proposal in 1848. It took over 70 years for women to win the right to vote.

Declaration of Sentiments

When, in the course of human events, it becomes necessary for one portion of the family of man to assume among the people of the earth a position different from that which they have hitherto occupied, but one to which the laws of nature and of nature's God entitle them, a decent respect to the opinions of mankind requires that they should declare the causes that impel them to such a course.

We hold these truths to be self-evident: that all men and women are created equal; that they are endowed by their Creator with certain **inalienable rights**, that among these are life, liberty, and the pursuit of happiness; that to secure these rights governments are instituted, deriving their just powers from the consent of the governed. Whenever any form of government becomes destructive of these ends; it is the right of those who suffer from it to refuse **allegiance** to it, and to insist upon the institution of a new government, laying its foundation on such principles, and organizing its powers in such form, as to them shall seem most likely to effect their safety and happiness. **Prudence** indeed, will dictate that government long established should not be changed for light and **transient** causes; and accordingly all experience hath shown that mankind are more disposed to suffer, while evils are sufferable, than to right themselves by abolishing the forms to which they were accustomed. But when a long train of abuses and **usurpations** pursuing invariably the same object **evinces** a design to reduce them under absolute **despotism** it is their duty to throw off such government, and to provide new guards for their future security. Such has been the patient sufferance of the women under this government, and such is now the necessity which constrains them to demand the equal station to which they are entitled.

The history of mankind is a history of repeated injuries and usurpations on the part of man toward woman, having in direct object the establishment of an absolute **tyranny** over her. To prove this, let facts be submitted to a candid world.

He has never permitted her to exercise her inalienable right to the **elective franchise**.

He has compelled her to submit to laws, in the formation of which she had no voice.

He has withheld from her rights which are given to the most ignorant and degraded men—both natives and foreigners.

Having deprived her of this first right of a citizen, the elective franchise, thereby leaving her without representation in the halls of legislation, he has oppressed her on all sides.

Inalienable rights: Rights that cannot be taken or given away.

Allegiance: Loyalty to a government, person, or idea.

Prudence: Good judgment or common sense.

Transient: Passing quickly.

Usurpations: Wrongfully taking control or taking charge.

Evince: To reveal or show.

Despotism: A ruling power that is abusive or unfair.

Tyranny: Oppressive power.

Elective franchise: The right to vote and be represented in government.

He has made her, if married, in the eye of the law, civilly dead.

He has taken from her all right in property, even to the wages she earns.

He has made her, morally, an irresponsible being, as she can commit many crimes with **impunity** provided they be done in the presence of her husband. In the covenant of marriage, she is compelled to promise obedience to her husband, he becoming to all intents and purposes, her master—the law giving him power to deprive her of her liberty, and to administer **chastisement**.

He has so framed the laws of divorce, as to what shall be the proper causes, and in case of separation, to whom the guardianship of the children shall be given, as to be wholly regardless of the happiness of women—the law, in all cases, going upon a false **supposition** of the supremacy of man, and giving all power into his hands.

After depriving her of all rights as a married woman, if single, and the owner of property, he has taxed her to support a government which recognizes her only when her property can be made profitable to it.

He has monopolized nearly all the profitable employments, and from those she is permitted to follow, she receives but a scanty **renumeration**. He closes against her all the avenues to wealth and distinction which he considers most honorable to himself. As a teacher of theology, medicine, or law, she is not known.

He has denied her the facilities for obtaining a thorough education, all colleges being closed against her.

He allows her in Church, as well as State, but a subordinate position, claiming **Apostolic** authority for her exclusion from the ministry, and, with some exceptions, from any public participation in the affairs of the Church.

He has created a false public sentiment by giving to the world a different code of morals for men and women,

Impunity: Freedom from punishment.

Chastisement: Punishment.

Supposition: A belief or an opinion.

Renumeration: Payment for services.

Apostolic: Relating to the teachings of the apostles, or missionaries, of the New Testament (that part of the Christian Bible covering events believed to have occurred after the birth of Jesus Christ).

by which moral delinquencies which exclude women from society, are not only tolerated, but deemed of little account in man.

He has usurped the prerogative of **Jehovah** himself, claiming it as his right to assign for her a sphere of action, when that belongs to her conscience and to her God.

He has endeavored, in every way that he could, to destroy her confidence in her own powers, to lessen her self-respect, and to make her willing to lead a dependent and **abject** life.

Now, in view of this entire **disfranchisement** of one-half the people of this country, their social and religious degradation—in view of the unjust laws above mentioned, and because women do feel themselves **aggrieved**, oppressed, and fraudulently deprived of their most sacred rights, we insist that they have immediate admission to all the rights, and privileges which belong to them as citizens of the United States.

In entering upon the great work before us, we anticipate no small amount of misconception, misrepresentation, and ridicule; but we shall use every **instrumentality** within our power to effect our object. We shall employ agents, circulate **tracts**, petition the State and National legislatures, and endeavor to enlist the pulpit and the press in our behalf. We hope this Convention will be followed by a series of Conventions embracing every part of the country.

WHEREAS, The great **precept** of nature is **conceded** to be, that "man shall pursue his own true and substantial happiness." [British law expert Sir William] Blackstone in his Commentaries [Commentaries on the Laws of England] remarks, that this law of Nature being **coeval** with mankind, and dictated by God himself, is of course superior in obligation to any other. It is binding over all the globe, in all countries and at all times; no human laws are of any validity if contrary to this, and such of them as are valid, derive all their force, and all their validity, and all their authority, **mediately** and immediately, from this original; therefore,

Jehovah: Another word for God.

Abject: Low and without hope.

Disfranchisement: To be deprived of one's legal rights, especially the right to vote.

Aggrieved: Offended or wronged.

Instrumentality: Any tool or action that helps achieve a goal.

Tracts: Booklets or pamphlets that discuss a political or religious point.

Precept: An idea or principle.

Conceded: Accepted, acknowledged, or granted.

Coeval: Of the same age or, in this case, occurring since the beginning of humanity.

Mediately: Indirectly.

Stanton

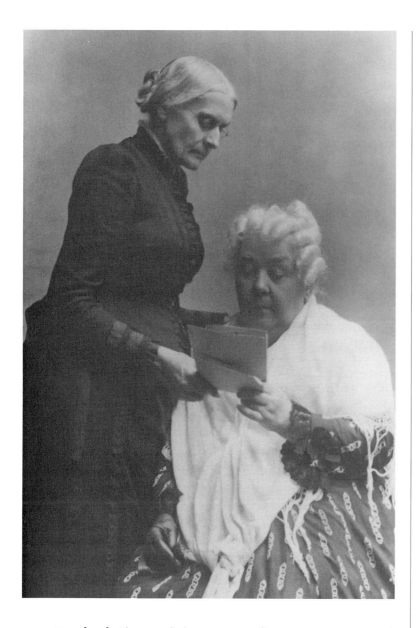

Resolved, That such laws as conflict, in any way, with the true and substantial happiness of woman, are contrary to the great precept of nature and of no validity, for this is "superior in obligation to any other."

Resolved, That all laws which prevent woman from occupying such a station in society as her conscience shall dictate, or which place her in a position inferior to that of man, are *contrary to the great precept of nature, and therefore of no force or authority.*

Resolved, That woman is man's equal, was intended to be so by the Creator, and the highest good of the race demands that she should be recognized as such.

Resolved, That the women of this country ought to be enlightened in regard to the laws under which they live, that they may no longer **publish** their degradation by declaring themselves satisfied with their present condition, nor their ignorance, by asserting that they have all the rights they want.

Resolved, That inasmuch as man, while claiming for himself intellectual superiority, does accord to woman moral superiority, it is pre-eminently his duty to encourage her to speak and teach, as she has an opportunity, in all religious assemblies.

Resolved, That the same amount of virtue, delicacy, and refinement of behavior that is required of woman in the social state, should also be required of man, and the same **transgressions** should be visited with equal severity on both man and woman.

Resolved, That the objection of indelicacy and impropriety, which is so often brought against woman when she addresses a public audience, comes with a very ill-grace from those who encourage, by their attendance, her appearance on the stage, in the concert, or in the feats of the circus.

Resolved, That woman has too long rested satisfied in the circumscribed limits which corrupt customs and a perverted application of the Scriptures have marked out for her, and that it is time she should move in the enlarged sphere which her great Creator has assigned her.

Resolved, That it is the duty of the women of this country to secure for themselves their sacred right to the elective franchise.

Resolved, That the equality of human rights results necessarily from the fact of the identity of the race in capabilities and responsibilities.

Publish: Make known.
Transgressions: Violations of the law.

Elizabeth Cady Stanton

Elizabeth Cady Stanton (1815-1902) was born and raised in Johnstown, New York, where her father was a judge on the New York Supreme Court. As a child, she was encouraged to develop her interest in law and her skills in debate. She attended Johnstown Academy, a boys' school, where she won first prize in Greek. Because women were not admitted to any U.S. colleges in the early nineteenth century, Stanton attended Emma Willard's female academy in Troy, New York, graduating in 1832. Eight years later, in 1840, she married abolitionist Henry B. Stanton. Together, they had seven children.

Resolved, therefore, That, being invested by the Creator with the same capabilities, and the same consciousness of responsibility for their exercise, it is demonstrably the right and duty of woman, equally with man, to promote every righteous cause by every righteous means; and especially in regard to the great subjects of morals and religion, it is self-evidently her right to participate with her brother in teaching them, both in private and in public, by writing and by speaking, by any instrumentalities proper to be used, and in any assemblies proper to be held; and this being a self-evident truth growing out of the divinely implanted principles of human nature, any custom or authority adverse to it, whether modern or wearing the **hoary** sanction of antiquity is to be regarded as a self-evident falsehood, and at war with mankind.

Resolved, That the speedy success of our cause depends upon the zealous and untiring efforts of both men and women,

Hoary: Gray or white with age.

for the overthrow of the monopoly of the pulpit, and for the securing to women an equal participation with men in the various trades, professions, and commerce. (Stanton et al., pp. 70-73)

What happened next...

In August of 1848, two weeks after the Seneca Falls convention, a larger meeting was held in Rochester, New York. The attendees of this convention approved the Declaration of Sentiments, then passed a slightly different set of resolutions that also included the right to vote. The Seneca Falls and Rochester conventions attracted a considerable amount of negative attention. Many leading clergymen and politicians wrote to newspapers claiming that women were unfit to vote. This ridicule and criticism intimidated many of the people who had signed the declaration and led them to withdraw their signatures.

Following the conventions of 1848, Stanton became known as a leader of the women's rights movement. She wrote to many women throughout the country, helping them prepare for their own local meetings and assemblies. Stanton's work for women's rights and abolition lasted through America's Civil War (1861-1865), a bloody conflict that divided the northern and southern states along social and political lines. She broke with abolitionists after slavery ended in 1865 because they championed voting rights for blacks but not for women.

In 1869 Stanton and renowned women's leader Susan B. Anthony founded the National Woman Suffrage Association (NWSA). Stanton served as president every year until 1890, when NWSA merged with another leading suffrage group to become the National American Woman Suffrage Association.

Did you know...

• The site of the first women's rights convention is now the Seneca Falls National Park.

- The table where Mott, Stanton, and three other women met and decided to plan the first women's rights convention is on display at the Smithsonian Institute in Washington, D.C.

- Charlotte Woodward was the only woman who attended the 1848 convention and lived to vote in the presidential election of 1920.

For Further Reading

Faber, Doris. *Oh, Lizzie! The Life of Elizabeth Cady Stanton.* New York: Lothrop, Lee & Shepard, 1972.

Flexner, Eleanor. *Century of Struggle: The Woman's Rights Movement in the United States.* Revised edition. Cambridge, Massachusetts: Belknap/Harvard University Press, 1975.

Gleiter, Jan, and Kathleen Thompson. *Elizabeth Cady Stanton.* Raintree, 1988.

Stanton, Elizabeth Cady, Susan B. Anthony, and Matilda Joslyn Gage, eds. *History of Woman Suffrage.* Vol. I. New York: Arno Press, 1969.

The Rights of Women

Newspaper article written by Frederick Douglass
Published in The North Star
July 28, 1848

Newspapers published in small U.S. towns and cities in the mid-1800s typically provided hostile, mocking reports on the first women's rights conventions at Seneca Falls and Rochester, New York. In fact, the ridicule was so loud and so constant across the Northeast that many women who had signed the convention resolutions asked to have their names removed. In what would become a pattern for news coverage of future women's rights conventions, abolitionist (anti-slavery) newspapers were the only publications willing to voice support.

The leading abolitionist newspaper, *The North Star,* was one of the few publications that championed women's rights. Its publisher, Frederick Douglass, was a famous African American leader in the antislavery movement who demonstrated a firm commitment to the goal of equality for women as well as slaves. Douglass attended the Seneca Falls Convention himself and was the only organizer who approved of Elizabeth Cady Stanton's controversial proposal demanding suffrage, or the right to vote, for women. In fact, it is possible that without Dou-

Fifteenth Amendment

Proposed in February, 1869
Ratified in March, 1870

After the Fourteenth Amendment was ratified in July 1868, many abolitionists and Republican leaders believed more specific legislation was needed to ensure the voting rights of newly freed black men. While the previous amendment penalized states that withheld voting privileges from black men, the Fifteenth Amendment directly ordered states to grant voting rights to former male slaves.

The American Equal Rights Association (AERA), a group of abolitionists and women's rights leaders, hotly debated whether to oppose or support an amendment that did not include voting rights for women. At a meeting in May 1869, Frederick Douglass, a leading abolitionist and former slave who had wholeheartedly supported women's suffrage at the 1848 Seneca Falls Convention, spoke about the need to secure voting rights for black men—even at the expense of securing voting rights for women. When another participant suggested that black women had received the same abuse as black men, Douglass reportedly replied, "Yes, yes, yes; it is true of the black woman, but not because she is a woman, but because she is black."

AMENDMENT XV

Section 1. The right of the citizens of the United States to vote shall not be denied or abridged by the United States or by any state, on account of race, color, or previous condition of servitude.

glass's support, Stanton might never have put forward her resolution for women's suffrage.

Things to Remember While Reading "The Rights of Women":

- Douglass completely supports and defends the idea that women are entitled to equal rights.

- He points out that other abolitionists view the idea of women's rights as absurd and admits that by backing women in their fight for equality, he may in fact lose supporters.

- Notice the linkage of black rights and women rights into one goal—human freedom. This concept of human rights appears again after the Civil War, when former abolitionists and leaders of the women's movement try to avoid splitting over voting rights for freed black men versus women.

The Rights of Women

*One of the most interesting events of the past week, was the holding of what is technically styled a Woman's Rights Convention at Seneca Falls. The speaking, addresses, and resolutions of this extraordinary meeting were almost **wholly** conducted by women; and although they evidently felt themselves in a novel position, it is but simple justice to say that their whole proceedings were characterized by marked ability and dignity. No one present, we think, however much he might be disposed to differ from the views advanced by the leading speakers on that occasion, will fail to give them credit for brilliant talents and excellent **dispositions**. In this meeting, as in other deliberative assemblies, there were frequent differences of opinion and animated discussion; but in no case was there the slightest absence of good feeling and **decorum**. Several interesting documents setting forth the rights as well as grievances of women were read. Among these was a Declaration of Sentiments, to be regarded as the basis of a grand movement for attaining the civil, social, political, and religious rights of women. We should not do justice to our own convictions, or to the excellent persons connected with this infant movement, if we did not in this connection offer a few remarks on the general subject which the Convention met to consider and the objects they seek to attain. In doing so, we are not **insensible** that the bare mention of this truly important subject in any other than terms of **contemptuous** ridicule and scornful disfavor, is likely to excite against us the fury of bigotry and the folly of prejudice. A discussion of the rights of animals would be regarded with far more **complacency** by many of what*

Wholly: Entirely; completely.

Dispositions: In this case, the women's character.

Decorum: Proper behavior.

Insensible: Unaware.

Contemptuous: Showing disrespect.

Complacency: Acceptance; self-satisfaction.

are called the wise and the good of our land, than would be a discussion of the rights of women. It is, in their estimation, to be guilty of evil thoughts, to think that woman is entitled to equal rights with man. Many who have at last made the discovery that the negroes have some rights as well as other members of the human family, have yet to be convinced that women are entitled to any. Eight years ago a number of persons of this description actually abandoned the anti-slavery cause, lest by giving their influence in that direction they might possibly be giving **countenance** to the dangerous **heresy** that woman, in respect to rights, stands on equal footing with man. In the judgment of such persons the American slave system, with all its **concomitant** horrors, is less to be **deplored** than this wicked idea. It is perhaps needless to say, that we cherish little sympathy for such sentiments or respect for such prejudices. Standing as we do upon the **watch-tower** of human freedom, we can not be **deterred** from an expression of our **approbation** of any movement, however humble, to improve and elevate the character of any members of the human family. While it is impossible for us to go into this subject at length, and dispose of the various objections which are often urged against such a doctrine as that of female equality, we are free to say that in respect to political rights, we hold woman to be justly entitled to all we claim for man. We go farther, and express our conviction that all political rights which it is **expedient** for man to exercise, it is equally so for woman. All that distinguishes man as an intelligent and accountable being, is equally true of woman; and if that government only is just which governs by the free consent of the governed, there can be no reason in the world for denying to woman the exercise of the elective franchise, or a hand in making and administering the laws of the land. Our doctrine is that "right is of no sex." We therefore bid the women engaged in this movement our humble **Godspeed**. (Reprinted in Stanton et al., pp. 74-75)

Countenance: Appearance of approval.

Heresy: An opinion that goes against generally accepted beliefs.

Concomitant: Accompanying.

Deplored: Regretted.

Watch-tower: A lookout tower.

Deterred: Prevented.

Approbation: Praise.

Expedient: Advisable or practical.

Godspeed: A wish for success.

Frederick Douglass

Abolitionist and journalist Frederick Douglass (c. 1817-1895) was born to an enslaved mother and white father in Tuckahoe, Maryland. He became one the leading orators and abolitionists of the 1800s. After escaping to freedom in 1838, he changed his name from Frederick Augustus Washington Bailey to Frederick Douglass to avoid capture. Douglass delivered his first public speech before the Massachusetts Anti-Slavery Society in 1841, where he described what freedom meant to him. He so impressed the society's members that they hired him as a public lecturer. In 1847 Douglass started *The North Star,* one of the most influential newspapers of the abolitionist movement. He is remembered as a key figure in the fight for female equality.

What happened next...

Douglass continued his support of both abolitionism and women's rights throughout the 1850s. During the Civil War (1861-1865) he helped recruit regiments of black soldiers for the Union Army. After the war Douglass and others were divided over the question of whether to support voting rights for women as well as for freed black men. The creation of the American Equal Rights Association in 1866 united former abolitionists and women right's leaders for a short period of time. At first both groups were willing to support the concept of universal suffrage. However, the proposal and then adoption of the Fourteenth and Fifteenth amendments caused a formal split between the parties. (The Fourteenth Amendment guarantees due process and equal protection under the law; the Fifteenth

Amendment gave freed black men the right to vote.) In spite of these disagreements, Douglass actively worked for women's rights throughout his life. In fact, he had just returned home after attending a suffrage meeting in Washington, D.C., when he died in 1895.

Did you know...

- According to some sources, Douglass chose his free name based on a character in Sir Walter Scott's narrative *Lady of the Lake.*

- During the 1840s Douglass protested segregated trains and created quite a stir by sitting in the cars reserved for whites. He also campaigned against segregated churches that permitted blacks to attend services only after white members had left.

- Douglass's home in Rochester, New York, was a station on the Underground Railroad (a secret system that helped runaway slaves from the South reach freedom in the North).

- Toward the end of his life, Douglass served as U.S. minister to Haiti (1889-91).

For Further Reading

Bennett, Evelyn. *Frederick Douglass and the War against Slavery.* Brookfield, Connecticut: Millbrook Press, 1933.

Foner, Philip S., ed. *Frederick Douglass on Women's Rights.* Westport, Connecticut: Greenwood Press, 1976.

Stanton, Elizabeth Cady, Susan B. Anthony, and Matilda Joslyn Gage, eds. *History of Woman Suffrage.* Vol I. Originally published in 1881. Reprinted. New York: Arno Press, 1969.

Ain't I a Woman?

Presented by Sojourner Truth
1851 Woman's Rights Convention
Akron, Ohio
May 28-29, 1851

After the first women's rights conventions held at Seneca Falls and Rochester, New York, in 1848, over a year passed before another meeting was organized. Finally, in 1850, another convention took place at a church in Salem, Ohio. In an unusual move, women organizers decided to ban men from speaking at the meeting. This controversial action was not repeated at the numerous conventions that followed Salem and did not reflect the typically supportive relationship between male and female organizers. In fact, the call, or invitation, for the First National Woman's Rights Convention held in 1850 was signed by many male leaders of the antislavery movement, including William Lloyd Garrison.

The 1850 convention brought national attention to many of the leaders of the emerging women's movement, such as Paulina Wright Davis, Lucretia Mott, Angelina Grimké, Lucy Stone, and Ernestine Rose. The convention also attracted new members, including Sojourner Truth, a former slave and powerful abolitionist. In support of Truth's attendance, two of the resolutions adopted by the convention expressed support for equality before the law—regardless of sex or color.

Truth had been active in the abolitionist movement since 1843, when she was living at a utopian community in Northampton, Massachusetts. Popular in the mid-1800s, utopian communities consisted of schools, farms, and housing organized by people who sought to create their own perfect society. In the late 1840s Truth traveled extensively throughout the Midwest, becoming one of the most popular speakers of her time at religious revivals and abolitionist rallies.

Truth delivered her most famous speech at the Second Women's Rights Convention held in Akron, Ohio, in 1851. When none of the women organizers could silence the hecklers in the audience, she stepped forward and, against some of the organizers' advice, was invited to speak by the convention president, Frances D. Gage. Truth, who was an imposing figure at nearly six feet tall, gave an electrifying speech that turned the loud jeers of the audience into cheers of support.

Despite audience opposition, convention president Frances D. Gage encouraged Truth to give her "Ain't I a Woman?" speech.

Things to Remember While Reading "Ain't I a Woman?":

- Truth was a famous lecturer in her day because of the honesty of her observations and the persuasiveness of her convictions.

- Notice several of the white female convention organizers feared that associating with a controversial black abolitionist leader would harm their movement.

- Gage's nervousness over her new role as president of the convention is understandable; most women activists of her era were inexperienced in the role of political leadership.

- Truth silenced two common sources of opposition frequently present at women's rights conventions: members of the clergy and rowdy male hecklers who enjoyed trying to intimidate women speakers.

- She points out that society had not given black women the same status as white women. For example, female slaves were expected to do hard physical labor; they were not viewed as the weaker sex, in need of protection.

Ain't I a Woman?

(As recalled by Frances D. Gage, who presided over the 1851 Woman's Rights Convention held in Akron, Ohio)

*The leaders of the movement trembled on seeing a tall, **gaunt** black woman in a gray dress and white turban, **surmounted** with an **uncouth** sun-bonnet, march deliberately into the church, walk with the air of a queen up the aisle, and take her seat upon the pulpit steps. A buzz of **disapprobation** was heard all over the house, and there fell on the listening ear, "An abolition affair!" "Woman's rights and niggers!" "I told you so!" "Go it, darkey!"*

*I chanced on that occasion to wear my first **laurels** in public life as president of the meeting. At my request order was restored, and the business of the Convention went on. Morning, afternoon, and evening exercises came and went. Through all these sessions old Sojourner, quiet and **reticent** ... sat crouched against the wall on the corner of the pulpit stairs, her sun-bonnet shading her eyes, her elbows on her knees, her chin resting upon her broad, hard palms. At intermission she was busy selling the "Life of Sojourner Truth," a narrative of her own strange and adventurous life. Again and again, **timorous** and trembling ones came to me and said, with earnestness, "Don't let her speak, Mrs. Gage, it will ruin us. Every newspaper in the land will have our cause mixed up with abolition and niggers, and we shall be utterly denounced." My only answer was, "We shall see when the time comes...."*

Gaunt: Being thin or lean.
Surmounted: Stood at the top of.
Uncouth: Strange in shape or appearance.
Disapprobation: Disapproval.
Laurels: Honor.
Reticent: Tendency to be silent.
Timorous: Timid or fearful.

There were very few women in those days who dared to "speak in meeting"; and the **august** teachers of the people were seemingly getting the better of us, while the boys in the galleries, and the sneerers among the pews, were hugely enjoying the **discomfiture**, as they supposed, of the "strong-minded." Some of the tender-skinned friends were on the point of losing dignity, and the atmosphere **betokened** a storm. When, slowly from her seat in the corner rose Sojourner Truth, who, till now, had scarcely lifted her head. "Don't let her speak!" gasped half a dozen in my ear. She moved slowly and solemnly to the front, laid her old bonnet at her feet, and turned her great speaking eyes to me. There was a hissing sound of disapprobation above and below. I rose and announced "Sojourner Truth," and begged the audience to keep silence for a few moments.

The **tumult** subsided at once, and every eye was fixed on this almost **Amazon** form, which stood nearly six feet high, head erect, and eyes piercing the upper air like one in a dream. At her first word there was a profound hush. She spoke in deep tones, which, though not loud, reached every ear in the house, and away through the throng at the doors and windows.

"Well, children, where there is so much racket there must be something out of kilter. I think that between the niggers of the South and the women of the North, all talking about rights, the white men will be in a fix pretty soon. But what's all this here talking about?

"That man over there say that women needs to be helped into carriages, and lifted over ditches, and to have the best place everywhere. Nobody ever helps me into carriages, or over mud-puddles, or gives me any best place!" And raising herself to her full height, and her voice to a pitch like rolling thunder, she asked, "And ain't I a woman? Look at me! Look at my arm! (and she bared her right arm to the shoulder, showing her tremendous muscular power). I have ploughed, and planted, and gathered into barns, and no man could head me! And ain't I a woman? I could work as much and eat as much as a

August: Marked by dignity or magnificence.

Discomfiture: Embarrassment.

Betokened: Hinted or showed.

Tumult: Riot.

Amazon: A member of a mythical race of female warriors.

man—when I could get it—and bear the lash as well! And ain't I a woman? I have borne thirteen children, and seen them most all sold off to slavery, and when I cried out with my mother's grief, none but Jesus heard me! And ain't I a woman?

"Then they talks about this thing in the head; what does they call it?" ("Intellect," whispered some one near.) "That's it, honey. What's that got to do with women's rights or niggers' rights? If my cup won't hold but a pint, and yours holds a quart, wouldn't you be mean not to let me have my little half-measure full?" And she pointed her **significant finger,** and sent a keen glance at the ministers who had made the argument. The cheering was long and loud.

"Then that little man in black there, he say women can't have as much rights as men, because Christ wasn't a woman! Where did your Christ come from?" Rolling thunder couldn't have stilled that crowd, as did those deep, wonderful tones, as she stood there with outstretched arms and eyes of fire. Raising her voice still louder, she repeated, "Where did your Christ come from? From God and a woman! Man had nothing to do with Him." Oh, what a rebuke that was to that little man.

Turning again to another **objector,** she took up the defense of Mother Eve. I can not follow her through it all. It was pointed, and witty, and solemn; **eliciting** at almost every sentence deafening applause; and she ended by asserting: "If the first woman God ever made was strong enough to turn the world upside down all alone, these women together (and she glanced her eye over the platform) ought to be able to turn it back, and get it right side up again! And now they is asking to do it, the men better let them." Long-continued cheering greeted this. "**Obliged** to you for hearing on me, and now old Sojourner hasn't got nothing more to say."

Amid roars of applause, she returned to her corner, leaving more than one of us with streaming eyes, and hearts beating with gratitude. She had taken us up in her strong arms and carried us safely over the **slough** of difficulty turning the whole tide in our favor. I have never in my life seen anything like

Significant finger:
Index finger.
Objector: Someone who disapproves or objects.
Eliciting: Bringing out.
Obliged: Put in one's debt by a favor.
Slough: Mucky mud or swamp.

Sojourner Truth

Sojourner Truth (c. 1797-1883), born Isabella Baumfree in Hurley, New York, spent the first 30 years of her life as a slave, receiving abusive treatment from her owners. She gave birth to 13 children, most of whom were sold into slavery. Sometime in 1827 she escaped—either by running away and then being taken in by the family of Isaac Van Wagener, or by being sold to Van Wagener, who then set her free. Either way, she was very grateful to the Van Wagener family for her freedom and for a while even took their name. She moved to New York City in 1829, joined an evangelical group, and began her career as a preacher. Disillusioned, she left the city in 1843 to launch her own spiritual mission. She changed her name to Sojourner Truth and began traveling throughout the country, speaking first as a religious preacher and then on behalf of abolitionist causes and the fight for women's rights.

the magical influence that subdued the mobbish spirit of the day, and turned the sneers and jeers of an excited crowd into notes of respect and admiration. Hundreds rushed up to shake hands with her, and congratulate the glorious old mother, and bid her **God-speed** on her mission of "testifying again concerning the wickedness of this here people." (Stanton et al., pp. 115-117)

God-speed: A wish for success.

What happened next...

After her appearance at the Akron Convention, Truth went on to become one of the most well-known supporters of female equality. Encouraged by feminist, activist, and antislavery organizer Lucretia Mott and other women leaders, Truth continued to speak at women's rights meetings for the rest of her life. Abolitionists and proponents of women's rights worked together during the rest of the 1850s, the decade leading up to the Civil War. However, after the war ended, the two groups split over the Fifteenth Amendment, which granted freed black men—but not women—the right to vote.

Did you know...

- Unable to read or write, Truth published her autobiography, *Narrative of Sojourner Truth,* by dictating her life story to a writer named Olive Gilbert.

- Truth experienced mystic visions, which she believed came from God. It was such a vision that led her to change her name to Sojourner Truth and begin traveling across the country urging people to accept the teachings of the Bible. Her name was symbolic of her mission—the word *sojourn* means to stay in one place for a short period of time, and the teachings of the Bible are often referred to as *truths.*

- During the Civil War Truth helped integrate the streetcars in Washington, D.C., and met President Abraham Lincoln at the White House.

- After the war she worked for the National Freedman's Relief Association, helping many ex-slaves resettle in Kansas and Missouri.

For Further Reading

Lindstrom, Aletha Jane. *Sojourner Truth: Slave, Abolitionist, Fighter for Women's Rights.* New York: J. Messner, 1980.

Macht, Norman L. *Sojourner Truth.* New York: Chelsea Juniors, 1992.

Stanton, Elizabeth Cady, Susan B. Anthony, and Matilda Joslyn Gage, eds. *History of Woman Suffrage.* Vol. I. Originally published in 1881. Reprinted. New York: Arno Press, 1969.

How God Is Teaching the Nation

Presented by Anna E. Dickinson
Brooklyn Academy of Music
As reported in the New York Times
May 24, 1863

Albany, New York, was the site of the last women's rights convention to be held before the outbreak of the Civil War. Within a few short weeks of the meeting, which convened in February 1861, the South attacked Fort Sumter in Charleston, South Carolina. The leaders of the women's rights movement decided to temporarily suspend their activities so they could concentrate on the war effort. Many of these women were committed to ending slavery and believed that they should focus their energies on the Union cause: the war offered a chance for an end to slavery, and their contributions as patriots would make it clear that women, as loyal and useful citizens, deserved the right to vote.

The Civil War changed the lives of all Americans, particularly slaves and women. Women realized the value of organizing on a national basis, a tactic they had not practiced in their prewar women's rights activities. They became active in many relief efforts, including setting up hospitals, serving as nurses, raising funds for soldiers and their families, and helping

Thirteenth Amendment

Proposed January 31, 1865
Ratified December 6, 1865

Leaders of the women's rights movement decided to suspend their efforts at the outbreak of the Civil War so they could concentrate on the fight to end slavery. Many women became concerned that the Emancipation Proclamation issued by President Abraham Lincoln, which freed slaves living in the rebellious states, did not go far enough to secure freedom for all African Americans. A split eventually developed between former abolitionists who supported the right to vote for freed slaves and women leaders who favored universal suffrage, or the right to vote for women—of all colors—as well as men.

AMENDMENT XIII

Section 1. Neither slavery nor involuntary servitude, except as a punishment for a crime whereof the party shall have been duly convicted, shall exist within the United States, or any place subject to their jurisdiction.

Section 2. Congress shall have power to enforce this article by appropriate legislation.

to educate freed slaves. Since the Emancipation Proclamation only granted freedom to slaves living in rebellious states, the Woman's National Loyal League was founded with the goal of petitioning Congress to outlaw slavery in every state.

Anna Dickinson knew another way to influence government and politics—through the power of the spoken word. Since she couldn't vote for the candidates of her choice, she campaigned for them. She became the most famous female orator, or public speaker, during the Civil War and the first woman orator to work for a major political party. Her skills at persuasion, combined with her belief in the justness of the war, made her a popular speaker at Republican political rallies.

Dickinson stumped, or campaigned, on behalf of Republicans throughout New England in 1863. Party officials were impressed with her ability to calm the sometimes violent crowds of Northerners who were opposed to the war. Due to her youthfulness, her biting sarcasm, and her attractive appearance, Dickinson received less heckling and harassment than other speakers during the draft riots of 1863.

Out of their appreciation for all the campaigning she had done for them, the Republicans invited Dickinson to address Congress in January 1864. She was only 21 years old when she delivered a talk about the true meaning of the war to the joint Congress and President and Mrs. Lincoln. The *New York Times* recounted two of the fiery speeches she gave in support of the Union—one in Brooklyn and one in Washington, D.C.

Things to Remember While Reading "How God Is Teaching the Nation":

- Look for Dickinson's deep convictions, or beliefs, about the importance of emancipation (freedom from slavery).

- Notice her harsh disapproval of Copperheads, Northerners who favored negotiating a peace with the Confederates (southern forces) that would allow slavery to exist. The name Copperheads comes from Copperhead snakes, considered slithery and unreliable.

- Dickinson uses dramatic flair at the end of her speech at the Brooklyn Academy when she refers by name to some of the Union soldiers—including Winthrop, Ellsworth, Baker, Mitchell, and Berry—who had died in various battles of the Civil War.

How God Is Teaching the Nation

Miss Dickinson in Brooklyn. *The Brooklyn Academy of Music was filled to its utmost capacity Friday, with a brilliant audience, assembled to hear Miss ANNA E. DICKINSON speak on the subject, "How God is Teaching the Nation." The orator was introduced by T. TILTON [New York State newspaper editor, abolitionist, and advocate of women's rights], and was received with loud applause. God is teaching the nation, she said, that it is fighting the battle of Liberty—not of the Union of FRANK PIERCE [fourteenth president of the United States (1853-57). Pierce and other Democrats backed the Kansas Nebraska Act of 1854, which meant slavery was once again allowed to exist in the Kansas area. The renewed controversy between slavery and antislavery forces led the northern part of the Democratic party to split and form the new Republican party] and JAMES BUCHANAN [fifteenth president of the United States (1857-61). Buchanan was a Democrat who opposed slavery yet believed the states should be allowed to decide the issue individually. During his administration, he sought peace with the southern states at any cost], but for "Liberty throughout the land to all the people thereof." [Applause.] The founders of the Republic, in framing the Constitution, meant Liberty. The very spirit of the **instrument** was progressive. But how has this spirit been violated? By warring against weak nations and helpless Indians, by passing a Fugitive Slave law, by **winking** at the African Slave-trade, by suppressing free speech and a free Press, by shutting out free labor from the Territories, by persecuting every person who has dared to open his lips against the slave power. More than this has been done, and the nation at last unable to bear it, stood up in its dignity and said, "We will have no more of this." Then in 1860, President LINCOLN was elected, and because he represented a party that was opposed to the continuance of these evils, the South*

Instrument: Legal document.
Winking: Pretending not to notice.

Anna E. Dickinson

Anna Elizabeth Dickinson (1842-1932) was born in Philadelphia, Pennsylvania, to a widowed mother. She received scholarships to attend the Friends' Select School of Philadelphia. An avid reader, Dickinson was well known for expressing her own opinions forcefully. She gave her first public speech at the age of 18, when she addressed the Pennsylvania Anti-Slavery Society. After speaking in Philadelphia in 1861 concerning "Women's Rights and Wrongs," she received invitations to travel and lecture throughout New England. The following year she joined abolitionist William Lloyd Garrison's network of lecturers.

During the Civil War Dickinson was the most famous female orator, or public speaker, in the country. She gave numerous lectures supporting the abolitionist cause and is said to have earned $20,000 a year from lecturing—an enormous amount of money at the time—until the public finally tired of her fiery, sermonlike speeches toward the end of the 1880s.

rebelled and went out of the Union. Her peculiar **institution** could not coexist with Liberty, and Liberty was in the Union. This war, then, is a war for the preservation of the national unity. The South had, so far, succeeded, because it had been terribly in earnest; because no means had been left unemployed to accomplish its ends; because the North had been **endeavoring** to **conciliate** by a mistaken and hurtful **clemency**;...

Institution: Established custom or practice.

Endeavoring: Making an effort toward a particular goal.

Conciliate: To bring to agreement.

Clemency: Showing mercy or forgiveness.

*There are but two parties in the country to-day—patriots and traitors. The party called **Copperheads** are in favor of peace—peace on the old footing—but that can never be obtained. Copperhead assemblages should be broken up, even though it be done at the point of the bayonet. [Applause.]*

To-day, out of the din and smoke of the conflict, through anguish and misery unutterable, the nation has been brought to feel sympathy for the right, and reverence for justice. If black men are given a chance to save themselves, they will save us. Let these men earn their liberty, and they will secure everlastingly the liberty of the nation. [Applause.]

*We are fighting for Freedom. It is glorious to suffer and to die in such a cause. We have had WINTHROP, young and brave, filled with a sweet, manly love, his life given away; ELLSWORTH, young and brave, flashing out for a moment, then falling, the flag twisted about him and drenched with his blood; BAKER, precipitating his depleted lines against Ball's Bluff, leaving a monument to all coming time for fame and honor. South Carolina, sacred with MITCHELL'S dying face looking out from it. [Applause.] Men falling thick in the dust at Antietam; BERRY rushing forward at Chancellorsville; two hundred thousand others as brave, as strong, as earnest, yet unrecorded, offered up. This long line passes in solemn **array**, lifting up its voice to God, and cries out, "Avenge, avenge, avenge us, O Lord, Lord" and, dropping his hand on you, he waits for your answer. Men of the North, your weak regret is wasted; arise, and pay to Freedom and to them the debt, by following where they led the way. [Great applause.]*

After Miss DICKINSON had concluded, loud cries were made for Senator POMEROY, of Kansas, who was on the platform; but he declined speaking, excusing himself on the ground that it was the part of courtesy always to permit a woman to have the last word. (As reported in the New York Times, *May 24, 1863)*

Copperheads: *Northerners who favored negotiating peace with the South.*

Array: *In an orderly way.*

What happened next...

Dickinson campaigned actively on behalf of enfranchisement, or voting rights, for women after the Civil War. She was a popular figure on the lyceum circuit, which were associations that provided adult education through public lectures and concerts. Her subjects ranged from Reconstruction (the rebuilding of the nation after the Civil War) to her favorite topic, St. Joan of Arc (the French patriot who was burned at the stake for her anti-British beliefs). Dickinson's thunderous, moralizing style eventually lost popularity as the states tried to put the Civil War behind them. She later took up a new career and began writing and acting in numerous stage productions. Her most successful play, *An American Girl,* ran in 1880.

Did you know...

- At the age of 14, Dickinson had an article printed in the abolitionist newspaper *The Liberator,* published by William Lloyd Garrison.

- Dickinson was fired from her civil service job at the United States Mint of Philadelphia when she criticized Union General George B. McClellan concerning his unfortunate defeat to the southern forces at Ball's Bluff.

- Wendell Philips, the famous abolitionist, referred to Dickinson as "the young elephant sent forward to try the bridges to see if they were safe for older ones to cross" (Philips in *History of Woman Suffrage,* Vol II, p. 42).

For Further Reading

Chester, Giraud. *Embattled Maiden: The Life of Anna Dickinson.* New York: Putnam, 1951.

Stanton, Elizabeth Cady, Susan B. Anthony, and Matilda Joslyn Gage, eds. *History of Woman Suffrage.* Vol II. Originally published in 1881. Reprinted. New York: Arno Press, 1969.

Suffrage

Women's struggle to win suffrage—the right to vote—began in 1848, when a few hundred women gathered in Seneca Falls, New York, to discuss women's rights. However, the early suffragists were also active abolitionists who became increasingly focused on ending slavery in the pre-Civil War era. In fact, leaders of the women's rights movement agreed to suspend their activities during the war so that they could devote their full energies to the Union (Northern, or antislavery) cause.

After the Union victory and the abolition of slavery, the women's movement split over the passage of the Fourteenth and Fifteenth amendments. These amendments granted voting rights to freed black men, but not to women. In 1869 the **National Woman Suffrage Association** was formed by women who refused to work for the passage of these amendments and instead pledged to focus solely on women's rights. Later the same year the women and men who supported the amendments formed the **American Woman Suffrage Association**.

British philosopher **John Stuart Mill** helped instill much needed legitimacy into the American women's rights movement with the publication of his book *The Subjection of Women* in 1869. Mill's essay attracted attention on both sides of the Atlantic, and many copies were sold at statewide suffrage conventions. Both American and British suffragists adopted Mill's book as the definitive analysis of women's role in society.

In 1871 a flamboyant stockbroker named **Victoria C. Woodhull** created a national sensation when she alleged that women already had the right to vote under the provisions of the Fourteenth Amendment. Since the amendment protects the privileges of American citizenship, Woodhull argued that women as citizens should be entitled to vote. **Susan B. Anthony** also used this argument when she attempted to vote in the presidential elections of 1872 and was arrested. By 1875 the Supreme Court ruled that the Fourteenth Amendment did not grant women the right to vote. Anthony went on to devote the rest of her life to working for a federal amendment for women's suffrage.

Temperance leaders (those committed to outlawing the production, sale, and consumption of liquor) began to champion women's suffrage in the 1870s. **Frances E. Willard** first proposed the idea as "home protection," meaning that women needed the power of the ballot to protect their families from the ill effects of alcohol. By having a say in municipal and local elections, women could effectively vote down liquor licenses for taverns in their towns.

The social club movement also helped increase the momentum for women's suffrage. From the 1860s to the 1920s millions of women joined clubs centered around interests outside of the home. One important suffrage leader who had originally participated in both antislavery groups and women's clubs was **Julia Ward Howe**. As one of America's favorite patriots, Howe boosted the credibility of the women's rights movement. During the Civil War she had written *The Battle Hymn of the Republic,* which became the most popular war song of the Union forces. Howe was a founding member of the New England Women's Club, which was launched in 1868, and helped form the American Woman Suffrage Association the following year.

Ida B. Wells-Barnett was another suffrage figure who came from the women's club movement. Wells-Barnett, a famous journalist who led a national antilynching crusade, helped start the first black women's suffrage organization, the Alpha Suffrage Club, which was active in Chicago.

The two major suffrage organizations—the National Woman Suffrage Association and the American Woman Suffrage Association—coexisted for more than 20 years, reflecting different styles of political leadership. In 1890 they merged to become the National American Woman Suffrage Association (NAWSA). After serving as president of NAWSA for many years, Susan B. Anthony resigned in 1900 at the age of 80. She chose **Carrie Chapman Catt**, an experienced leader and suffrage worker, to be her successor. Catt led the suffrage movement through its final critical years. She also helped reorganize the two million members of NAWSA into the League of Women Voters in 1920, when passage of the **Nineteenth Amendment** (granting women the right to vote) appeared certain.

During World War I suffragists continued their activities. While America fought to promote democracy abroad, half its citizens were still not entitled to vote. Finally, President Woodrow Wilson gave his official support to the suffrage amendment. A bill allowing women the right to vote passed Congress in 1919 and received full ratification in 1920. After almost an entire century of struggle, American women had finally gained power at the ballot box. Only one woman who attended the 1848 Seneca Falls meeting lived long enough to vote: Charlotte Woodward voted in the presidential elections of 1920 when she was 93 years old.

The Subjection of Women

Written by John Stuart Mill
Published in 1869

For over 125 years since it was first published in 1869, John Stuart Mill's essay *The Subjection of Women* has been a landmark in the history of the women's rights movement. Mill, a prominent English philosopher and economist, wrote many influential books concerning political and social theory. While he was best known for his philosophical ideas, he also had an impact on England's political history. He served one term in Parliament (1865-68) and is remembered for introducing the first English legislation dealing with women's suffrage, or the right for women to vote. His work *The Subjection of Women* is a rigorous defense of equal rights for women.

While Mill's essay attracted attention on both sides of the Atlantic, the timing of its arrival in America was critical. During the difficult post-Civil War era, American suffragists had lost some of their strongest and earliest supporters. Frederick Douglass and other male abolitionists (antislavery activists) withdrew their support of women's voting rights in order to ensure black male suffrage. Mill's *Subjection of Women* gave the American women's rights movement a much-needed new source of support. Not only was Mill respected, he was a prominent *male* leader; his participation helped provide credibility to the women's cause.

Both English and American suffrage leaders quickly accepted Mill's essay as the authoritative analysis of women's position in society. At American suffrage conventions, organizers sold copies of it and referred to it in their speeches and articles. The older leaders—Elizabeth Cady Stanton, Sarah Grimké, and Lucretia Mott among them—especially appreciated Mill's work and discuss its impact in their autobiographies.

The British and American suffrage movements profoundly influenced each other. For example, Mill's wife, Harriet Taylor Mill, was inspired to publish one of the early English articles about women's rights after reading an account of the first American national women's rights convention held in Worcester, Massachusetts, in 1850. Mill also credits his wife with helping him develop the ideas represented in *The Subjection of Women.*

Mill began the first draft of his essay in 1860, a few years after his wife's death. However, he did not revise and publish it until after he retired from the House of Commons in 1868. Historians speculate that he intentionally excluded discussion of controversial topics such as divorce and child custody. He probably thought his chances of winning over opponents would be greater if he avoided the risk of scandal, so he refrained from challenging beliefs about marriage and the tradition of fathers receiving sole custody rights to their children after a divorce.

Things to Remember While Reading
The Subjection of Women:
- Mill is famous for his *rationalism,* the idea that a logical discussion can persuade or change deeply held, emotional beliefs. His writing shows both a strong commitment to his point of view and a degree of compassion for readers who might hold strong opposing views.

- Notice Mill's tone suggesting that a *reasonable* person could not dispute the truth that women are entitled to equal treatment.

- Look for where he argues that society's unfair legal, social, and political structure concerning women evolved unintentionally over time. He urges his readers to realize that women should have equality with men both politically and socially.

The Subjection of Women

The object of this Essay is to explain, as clearly as I am able, the grounds of an opinion which I have held from the very earliest period when I had formed any opinions at all on social or political matters, and which, instead of being weakened or modified, has been constantly growing stronger by the progress of reflection and the experience of life: That the principle which regulates the existing social relations between the two sexes—the legal subordination of one sex to the other—is wrong in itself, and now one of the chief hindrances to human improvement; and that it ought to be replaced by a principle of perfect equality, admitting no power or privilege on the one side, nor disability on the other.

*The very words necessary to express the task I have undertaken, show how **arduous** it is. But it would be a mistake to suppose that the difficulty of the case must lie in the insufficiency or **obscurity** of the grounds of reason on which my conviction rests. The difficulty is that which exists in all cases in which there is a mass of feeling to be **contended** against. So long as an opinion is strongly rooted in the feelings, it gains rather than loses in stability by having a **preponderating** weight of argument against it. For if it were accepted as a result of argument, the **refutation** of the argument might shake the solidity of the conviction; but when it rests solely on feeling, the worse it fares in argumentative contest, the more persuaded its adherents are that their feeling must have some deeper ground, which the arguments do not reach; and while the feeling remains, it is always throwing up fresh **entrenchments** of argument to repair any breach made in the old. And there are so*

Arduous: Difficult.
Obscurity: Remoteness.
Contended: Struggled or argued.
Preponderating: More important.
Refutation: Rejection; the act of proving something wrong or false.
Entrenchments: Defenses.

John Stuart Mill

John Stuart Mill (1806-1873) was born in London and educated at home by his father, Scottish philosopher James Mill. Young Mill learned Greek when he was three years old and Latin when he was eight. Following closely in his father's footsteps, he became a philosopher and economist, working at the British East India Company. Mill wrote many essays about political and social theory that remain famous for their clarity and thoroughness. He is perhaps best known for his work *On Liberty,* published in 1859. When his wife, Harriet Taylor Mill, died suddenly at Avignon, France, in 1858, Mill bought a villa near the cemetery where she was buried. He continued to live mainly in France for the rest of his life. He died in Avignon in 1873 at the age of 67.

many causes tending to make the feelings connected with this subject the most intense and most deeply-rooted of all those which gather round and protect old institutions and customs, that we need not wonder to find them as yet less undermined and loosened than any of the rest by the progress of the great modern spiritual and social transition; nor suppose that the **barbarisms** to which men cling longest must be less barbarisms than those which they earlier shake off.

In every respect the **burthen** is hard on those who attack an almost universal opinion. They must be very fortunate as well as unusually capable if they obtain a hearing at all. They

Barbarisms: Words or ideas that offend current standards of correctness.

Burthen: Burden; load.

*have more difficulty in obtaining a trial, than any other **litigants** have in getting a verdict. If they do **extort** a hearing, they are subjected to a set of logical requirements totally different from those exacted from other people. In all other cases, the burthen of proof is supposed to lie with the affirmative. If a person is charged with a murder, it rests with those who accuse him to give proof of his guilt, not with himself to prove his innocence.... But of none of these rules of evidence will the benefit be allowed to those who maintain the opinion I profess. It is useless for me to say that those who maintain the doctrine that men have a right to command and women are under an obligation to obey, or that men are fit for government and women unfit, are on the affirmative side of the question, and that they are bound to show positive evidence for the assertions, or submit to their rejection. It is equally **unavailing** for me to say that those who deny to women any freedom or privilege rightly allowed to men, having the double presumption against them that they are opposing freedom and recommending **partiality,** must be held to the strictest proof of their case, and unless their success be such as to exclude all doubt, the judgement ought to go against them. These would be thought good pleas in any common case; but they will not be thought so in this instance. Before I could hope to make any impression, I should be expected not only to answer all that has ever been said by those who take the other side of the question, but to imagine all that could be said by them—to find them in reasons, as well as answer all I find: and besides refuting all arguments for the affirmative, I shall be called upon for **invincible** positive arguments to prove a negative. And even if I could do all this, and leave the opposite party with a host of unanswered arguments against them, and not a single **unrefuted** one on their side, I should be thought to have done little; for a cause supported on the one hand by universal usage, and on the other by so great a preponderance of popular sentiment, is supposed to have a presumption in its favour, superior to any conviction which an appeal to reason has power to produce in any intellects but those of a high class....*

Litigants: Parties in a lawsuit.
Extort: To obtain by force.
Unavailing: Of no use.
Partiality: Bias; the favoring of one side more than another.
Invincible: Cannot be overcome.
Unrefuted: Not proven to be false.

Mill

*The generality of a practice is in some cases a strong presumption that it is, or at all events once was, **conducive** to **laudable** ends. This is the case, when the practice was first adopted, or afterwards kept up, as a means to such ends, and was grounded on experience of the mode in which they could be most effectually attained. If the authority of men over women, when first established, had been the result of a conscientious comparison between different modes of constituting the government of society; if, after trying various other modes of social organization—the government of women over men, equality between the two, and such mixed and divided modes of government as might be invented—it had been decided, on the testimony of experience, that the mode in which women are wholly under the rule of men, having no share at all in public concerns, and each in private being under the legal obligation of obedience to the man with whom she has associated her destiny, was the arrangement most conducive to the happiness and well-being of both; its general adoption might then be fairly thought to be some evidence that, at the time when it was adopted, it was the best: though even then the considerations which recommended it may, like so many other **primeval** social facts of the greatest importance, have subsequently, in the course of ages, ceased to exist. But the state of the case is in every respect the reverse of this. In the first place, the opinion in favour of the present system, which entirely subordinates the weaker sex to the stronger, rests upon theory only; for there never has been trial made of any other: so that experience, in the sense in which it is vulgarly opposed to theory, cannot be pretended to have pronounced any verdict. And in the second place, the adoption of this system of inequality never was the result of deliberation, or forethought, or any social ideas, or any notion whatever of ... the benefit of humanity or the good order of society. It arose simply from the fact that from the very earliest twilight of human society, every women (owing to the value attached to her by men, combined with her inferiority in muscular strength) was found in a state of bondage to some man.... And this, indeed, is what makes it strange to*

Conducive: To promote or assist.
Laudable: Worthy of praise.
Primeval: Primitive; relating to early ages.

ordinary ears, to hear it asserted that the inequality of rights between men and women has no other source than the law of the strongest. (Mill, pp. 427-33)

What happened next...

Mill's *Subjection of Women* won much praise from leaders in both the American and English women's rights movements during the last few decades of the nineteenth century and the early part of the twentieth century. At the dawn of the twenty-first century, people throughout the world still valued the ideals about which Mill wrote: the right to full equality and the right to justice in all forms of government. His descriptions of the obstacles to full equality and the reasons for discrimination continue to provide insight in understanding modern social and political systems.

Did you know...

- Even though she was 77 years old, the famous abolitionist and women's rights speaker Sarah Grimké sold 100 copies of Mill's book *The Subjection of Women* by going door to door throughout her town.

- Carrie Chapman Catt, a second generation American suffragist, wrote the introduction to the 1911 reprint of *The Subjection of Women.* Catt hoped the new edition would provide "untold value to the movement."

- American women won the right to vote in 1920, more than 50 years after Mill's book first appeared in 1869.

For Further Reading

Mill, John Stuart. *Three Essays.* Oxford: Oxford University Press, 1975.

Rossi, Alice S., ed., *The Feminist Papers: From Adams to de Beauvoir.* New York: Columbia University Press, 1973.

Address to the Judiciary Committee

Presented by Victoria C. Woodhull
U.S. House of Representatives
January 11, 1871

One of the early attempts to gain women's suffrage through federal action involved reinterpreting the U.S. Constitution. Francis Minor, an attorney from Missouri, was the first person to suggest that the Fourteenth Amendment—an outline of the privileges guaranteed to citizens—extended voting rights to women. Victoria C. Woodhull seized upon Minor's ideas, which he had published in the newspaper *The Revolution.* She sent a petition to Congress in 1870, and the House of Representatives invited her to personally present her argument to the Judiciary Committee on January 11, 1871.

Woodhull was already famous as America's first female stockbroker. In 1868 she and her sister, Tennessee Clafin, opened a brokerage firm on Wall Street in New York City with the help of financier Cornelius Vanderbilt. Their firm, Woodhull, Clafin, & Co., was quite successful; the sisters made a fortune for themselves. In 1870 they also began publishing their own magazine, *Woodhull and Clafin's Weekly,* which they used to promote many controversial ideas including women's suffrage and socialism.

The two major suffragist organizations in the United States, the National Woman Suffrage Association (NWSA) and the American Woman Suffrage Association (AWSA), did not fully trust Woodhull because of her unconventional ideas. However, the leaders of the NWSA attended Woodhull's congressional address and were so impressed with her speech that they invited her to attend their annual convention.

In response to Woodhull's address, the NWSA formed a special committee to educate women about the need to petition Congress. Susan B. Anthony went on a lecture tour informing women that the existing Constitution granted them the right to vote. Copies of Woodhull's address and other political brochures, known as tracts, flooded the country. Anthony and other leaders of the NWSA urged women to try to register and vote at their local polls.

Things to Remember While Reading the Address:
- Woodhull points out that the Constitution contains no mention of gender regarding voting rights.

- She argues that women fit the three conditions assuring the rights of citizenship as described in the Fifteenth Amendment, *that the privileges of citizenship can not be denied on account of race, color, or previous condition of servitude.*

- Notice the reference to the American Revolution concerning the issue of *no taxation without representation.* Woodhull finds fault in the practice of taxing women as if they are citizens but denying them the right to vote.

Address of Victoria C. Woodhull to the Judiciary Committee

The **sovereign** will of the people is expressed in our written Constitution, which is the supreme law of the land. The Constitution makes no distinction of sex. The Constitution defines a woman born or **naturalized** in the United States, and subject to the jurisdiction thereof, to be a citizen. It recognizes the right of citizens to vote. It declares that the right of citizens of the United States to vote shall not be denied or abridged by the United States or by any State on account of "race, color, or previous condition of servitude."

Women, white and black, belong to races, although to different races. A race of people comprises all the people, male and female. The right to vote can not be denied on account of race. All people included in the term race have the right to vote, unless otherwise prohibited. Women of all races are white, black, or some intermediate color. Color comprises all people, of all races and both sexes. The right to vote can not be denied on account of color. All people included in the term color have the right to vote unless otherwise prohibited....

Women, white and black, have from time immemorial groaned under what is properly termed in the Constitution "previous condition of servitude." Women are the equals of men before the law, and are equal in all their rights as citizens. Women are **debarred** from voting in some parts of the United States, although they are allowed to exercise that right elsewhere. Women were formerly permitted to vote in places where they are now debarred therefrom. The naturalization laws of the United States expressly provide for the naturalization of women. But the right to vote has only lately been definitely declared by the Constitution to be **inalienable,** under three distinct conditions—in all of which woman is clearly embraced.

The citizen who is taxed should also have a voice in the subject matter of taxation. "No taxation without representation" is a right which was fundamentally established at the very birth of our country's independence; and by what ethics does any free government impose taxes on women without giving them a voice upon the subject or a participation in the public declaration as to how and by whom these taxes shall be applied for common public use? Women are free to own and to control property, separate and free from males, and they are held responsible in their own proper persons, in every partic-

Debarred: Excluded.
Inalienable: Incapable of being surrendered or transferred.

Victoria C. Woodhull

Victoria C. Woodhull (1838-1927) was born in Homer, Ohio, to a family of traveling faith healers. Woodhull and her sister, Tennessee Clafin, were involved with spiritualism, the belief that it is possible to communicate with the spirits of people who have died. After becoming the first women to address Congress concerning women's right to vote, the sisters created a national scandal when they published the details of a married man's secret love affair in their newspaper, *Woodhull and Clafin's Weekly.* In 1877 they moved to England, married wealthy men, and became involved in numerous charities. Woodhull died at her country estate near Tewkesbury, Gloucestershire, when she was 89 years old.

ular, as well as men, in and out of court. Women have the same inalienable right to life, liberty, and the pursuit of happiness that men have. Why have they not this right politically, as well as men?

Women constitute a majority of the people of this country —they hold vast portions of the nation's wealth and pay a proportionate share of the taxes. They are **intrusted** with the most vital responsibilities of society; they bear, rear, and educate men; they train and **mould** their characters; they inspire the noblest impulses in men; they often hold the accumulated fortunes of a man's life for the safety of the family and as guardians of the infants, and yet they are debarred from uttering any opinion by public vote, as to the management by public servants of these interests; they are the secret counselors, the best advisers, the most devoted aids in the most

Intrusted: Entrusted.

Mould: To mold or shape.

trying periods of men's lives, and yet men shrink from trusting them in the common questions of ordinary politics. Men trust women in the market, in the shop, on the highway and railroad, and in all other public places and assemblies, but when they propose to carry a slip of paper with a name upon it to the polls, they fear them. Nevertheless, as citizens, women have the right to vote; they are part and parcel of that great element in which the sovereign power of the land had birth; and it is by **usurpation** only that men debar them from this right. The American nation, in its march onward and upward, can not publicly choke the intellectual and political activity of half its citizens by narrow **statutes.** The will of the entire people is the true basis of republican government, and a free expression of that will by the public vote of all citizens, without distinctions of race, color, occupation, or sex, is the only means by which that will can be ascertained. As the world has advanced into civilization and culture; as mind has risen in its **dominion** over matter; as the principle of justice and moral right has gained sway, and merely physical organized power has yielded thereto; as the might of right has supplanted the right of might, so have the rights of women become more fully recognized, and that recognition is the result of the development of the minds of men, which through the ages she has polished, and thereby heightened the **lustre** of civilization.

It was reserved for our great country to recognize by constitutional enactment that political equality of all citizens which religion, affection, and common sense should have long since accorded; it was reserved for America to sweep away the mist of prejudice and ignorance.... As the Constitution, in its paramount character, can only be read by the light of the established principle ... and as the subject of sex is not mentioned, and the Constitution is not limited either in terms or by necessary implication in the general rights of citizens to vote, this right can not be limited on account of anything in the spirit of inferior or previous enactments upon a subject which is not mentioned in the supreme law. A different construction would destroy a vested right in a portion of the citizens, and this no legislature has

Usurpation: *To wrongfully take authority.*

Statutes: *Laws.*

Dominion: *Authority.*

Lustre: *Brilliance or distinction.*

a right to do without compensation, and nothing can compensate a citizen for the loss of his or her suffrage—its value is equal to the value of life. Neither can it be presumed that women are to be kept from the polls as a mere police regulation: it is to be hoped, at least, that police regulations in their case need not be very active. The effect of the amendments to the Constitution must be to annul the power over this subject in the States, whether past, present, or future, which is contrary to the amendments. The amendments would even arrest the action of the Supreme Court in cases pending before it prior to their adoption, and operate as an absolute prohibition to the exercise of any other jurisdiction than merely to dismiss the suit....

Your **memorialist** complains of the existence of State laws, and **prays** Congress, by appropriate legislation, to declare them, as they are, annulled, and to give vitality to the Constitution under its power to make and alter the regulations of the States contravening the same.

It may be urged in opposition that the courts have power, and should declare upon this subject. The Supreme Court has the power, and it would be its duty so to declare the law: but the court will not do so unless a determination of such point as shall arise make it necessary to the determination of a controversy, and hence a case must be presented in which there can be no rational doubt. All this would subject the aggrieved parties to much **dilatory**, expensive and needless litigation, which your memorialist prays your honorable body to dispense with by appropriate legislation....

Therefore, believing firmly in the right of citizens to freely approach those in whose hands their destiny is placed under the Providence of God, your memorialist has frankly, but humbly, appealed to you, and prays that the wisdom of Congress may be moved to action in this matter for the benefit and the increased happiness of our beloved country. (Stanton et al., pp. 444-48)

Memorialist: *Person who has written a memorial or petition addressed to the government; in this case, Victoria C. Woodhull herself.*

Prays: *Requests.*

Dilatory: *Intended to cause delay.*

What happened next...

The women's rights movement eventually separated itself from Woodhull due to her support of "Free Love," a controversial, modernistic call for women's sexual equality. Woodhull felt it was unfair for society to hold men and women to different moral standards. As a solution, she recommended that men and women should be free to love each other outside of marriage. Newspapers harshly condemned her, and in response she used her own *Woodhull and Clafin's Weekly* to publish the details of a scandal involving Henry Ward Beecher, a famous minister and former president of the AWSA. Beecher was married and having an affair with the wife of prominent newspaper publisher Theodore Tilton. The backlash from this national scandal not only troubled the members of the women's rights movement but forced Woodhull and her sister to move to England in 1877.

Did you know...

- Woodhull was the first woman to run for president of the United States. In 1872 she received the endorsement of the Equal Rights Party, an organization she and others had formed when they broke away from the NWSA.

- In 1872 *Woodhull and Clafin's Weekly* published the first English translation of the *Communist Manifesto,* a political treatise originally written in German by leading nineteenth-century philosophers Karl Marx and Friedrich Engels. (Communism is a political and economic theory advocating the formation of a classless society through the communal ownership of all property.)

- While in her seventies, Woodhull became one of the early benefactors of aviation; in 1914 she offered a $5,000 prize to the pilot of the first transatlantic flight.

For Further Reading

Johnston, Johanna. *Mrs. Satan: The Incredible Saga of Victoria C. Woodhull.* New York: Putnam, 1967.

Papachristou, Judith. *Women Together.* New York: Alfred A. Knopf, 1976.

Stanton, Elizabeth Cady, Susan B. Anthony, Matilda Joslyn Gage, eds. *History of Woman Suffrage.* Vol II. Originally published in 1881. Reprinted. New York: Arno Press, 1969.

United States vs. Susan B. Anthony

Selections from transcripts of the trial
Rochester, New York, 1873

During the late 1860s and throughout the 1870s activists in the women's rights movement argued that the Fourteenth Amendment granted women as well as freed slaves the right to vote. Since this amendment included a description of the rights and privileges of U.S. citizens, women argued that they too were citizens of the States and should also be allowed to vote in elections. Small numbers of women attempted to register and vote across the country. In Vineland, New Jersey, 172 women cast their ballots in the 1868 presidential election—including four black women. And in 1879 elderly former abolitionists Sarah and Angelina Grimké, along with a group of 40 other women, voted in Hyde Park, Massachusetts, despite a harsh winter snowstorm.

The most famous court case concerning this political and legal tactic involved Susan B. Anthony, one of the greatest leaders of the women's rights movement. Anthony and a group of 16 women, including several Quakers, registered and voted in the presidential elections of 1872 in Rochester, New York. (Quakers, members of the Christian sect known as the Society of Friends,

In 1978 the Senate Banking Committee approved the "Susan B. Anthony" $1.00 coin.

lead lives of simplicity, tolerance, and peace.) After being arrested and set free on $1,000 bail, Anthony stumped (or rallied) for women's suffrage throughout Monroe County. She attracted so much attention and support with her lecture "Is It a Crime for a U.S. Citizen to Vote?" that the prosecuting attorney moved the trial to a neighboring county. With only three weeks before her court date, Anthony and another women's rights leader, Matilda Joslyn Gage, hit the campaign road again.

Anthony was an experienced political organizer who had been active in both the temperance (advocating complete abstinence from liquor) and antislavery causes. Her involvement with the temperance movement to outlaw liquor led her to realize that women did not have rights equal to those of men. When she attended a temperance rally in Albany, New York, in 1852, she was not allowed to speak because of her gender. Shortly after meeting Elizabeth Cady Stanton, one of the earliest leaders of the women's rights movement, Anthony became dedicated to fighting for women's equality.

Things to Remember While Reading
United States vs. Susan B. Anthony:

- Anthony suggests that people are sometimes justified in not obeying the law. She reminds the judge that many people violated the Civil War-era antifugitive laws by helping slaves escape to Canada.

- When the judge issues Anthony a $100 fine, she refuses to pay because she feels it is an unjust demand. Notice how the judge informs her that he will not force her to pay; this means she loses her chance to appeal the decision to the Supreme Court.

- Anthony points out that the judge refused to allow the jury to decide the verdict. It seems he followed improper procedures by ruling on the case himself in order to ensure the outcome.

- She mentions the debt she owes related to the bankruptcy of *The Revolution.* It took Anthony six years to pay off this $10,000 debt using the fees she earned from lecturing.

United States vs. Susan B. Anthony

The COURT: The prisoner will stand up. Has the prisoner anything to say why sentence shall not be pronounced?

Miss ANTHONY: Yes, your honor, I have many things to say; for in your ordered verdict of guilty, you have trampled underfoot every vital principle of our government. My natural rights, my civil rights, my political rights, are all alike ignored. Robbed of the fundamental privilege of citizenship, I am degraded from the status of a citizen to that of a subject; and not only myself individually, but all my sex, are, by your honor's verdict, doomed to political subjection under this so-called Republican government.

Judge HUNT: The Court can not listen to a rehearsal of arguments the prisoner's counsel has already consumed three hours in presenting.

Fourteenth Amendment

Proposed in April, 1866
Ratified in July, 1868

In July 1868 the Fourteenth Amendment was ratified, which penalized states that denied voting rights to black men. This amendment includes the term "he" specifically to exclude women, which is the first time a gender restriction appears in the Constitution in regards to voting rights.

AMENDMENT XIV

Section 1. All persons born or naturalized in the United States, and subject to the jurisdiction thereof, are citizens of the United States and of the state wherein they reside. No state shall make or enforce any law which shall abridge the privileges or immunities of citizens of the United States; nor shall any state deprive any person of life, liberty, or property without due process of law; nor deny to any person within its jurisdiction the equal protection of the law.

Section 2. When the right to vote at any election for the choice of electors for President and Vice President of the United States, representatives in Congress, the executive and judicial officers of a state, or the members of the legislature thereof, is denied to any of the male inhabitants of such state being of twenty-one years of age, and citizens of the United States, or in any way abridged, except for participation in rebellion or other crime, the basis of representation therein shall be reduced in the proportion which the number of such male citizens shall bear to the whole number of male citizens twenty-one years of age in such state.

Miss ANTHONY: May it please your honor, I am not arguing the question, but simply stating the reasons why sentence can not, in justice, be pronounced against me. Your denial of my citizen's right to vote is the denial of my right of consent as one of the governed, the denial of my right of representation as one of the taxed, the denial of my right to a trial by a jury of my peers as an offender against law, therefore, the denial of my sacred rights to life, liberty, property, and—

Judge HUNT: The Court can not allow the prisoner to go on.

Miss ANTHONY: But your honor will not deny me this one and only poor privilege of protest against this high-handed outrage upon my citizen's rights. May it please the Court to remember that since the day of my arrest last November, this is the first time that either myself or any person of my **disfranchised** class has been allowed a word of defense before judge or jury—

Judge HUNT: The prisoner must sit down; the Court can not allow it.

Miss ANTHONY: All my prosecutors, from the 8th Ward corner grocery politician, who entered the complaint, to the United States Marshal, Commissioner, District Attorney, District Judge, your honor on the bench, not one is my peer, but each and all are my political **sovereigns**; and had your honor submitted my case to the jury, as was clearly your duty, even then I should have had just cause of protest, for not one of those men was my peer; but, native or foreign, white or black, rich or poor, educated or ignorant, awake or asleep, sober or drunk, each and every man of them was my political superior; hence, in no sense, my peer. Even, under such circumstances, a commoner of England, tried before a jury of lords, would have far less cause to complain than should I, a woman, tried before a jury of men. Even my counsel, the Hon. Henry R. Selden, who has argued my cause so ably, so earnestly, so unanswerably before your honor, is my political sovereign. Precisely as no disfranchised person is entitled to sit upon a jury, and no woman is entitled to the franchise, so, none but a regularly admitted lawyer is allowed to practice in the courts, and no woman can gain admission to the bar—hence, jury, judge, counsel, must all be of the superior class.

Judge HUNT: The Court must insist—the prisoner has been tried according to the established forms of law.

Miss ANTHONY: Yes, your honor, but by forms of law all made by men, interpreted by men, administered by men, in favor of men, and against women; and hence, your honor's

Disfranchised: *Deprived of the right to vote.*
Sovereigns: *Absolute authorities.*

An Anthony lookalike leads a 1978 parade marking the 75th anniversary of the 19th Amendment.

ordered verdict of guilty, against a United States citizen for the exercise of "that citizen's right to vote," simply because that citizen was a woman and not a man. But … the same man-made forms of law declared it a crime punishable with $1,000 fine and six months' imprisonment, for you, or me, or any of us, to give a cup of cold water, a crust of bread, or a night's shelter to a panting fugitive as he was tracking his way to Canada. And every man or woman in whose veins coursed a drop of human sympathy violated that wicked law, reckless of consequences, and was justified in so doing. As then the slaves who got their freedom must take it over, or under, or through the unjust forms of law, precisely so now must women, to get their right to a voice in this Government, take it; and I have taken mine, and mean to take it at every possible opportunity.

 Judge HUNT: The Court orders the prisoner to sit down. It will not allow another word.

Miss ANTHONY: When I was brought before your honor for trial, I hoped for a broad and liberal interpretation of the Constitution and its recent amendments, that should declare all United States citizens under its protecting **aegis**—that should declare equality of rights the national guarantee to all persons born or **naturalized** in the United States. But failing to get this justice—failing, even, to get a trial by a jury not of my peers—I ask not leniency at your hands—but rather the full rigors of the law.

Judge HUNT: The Court must insist—(Here the prisoner sat down.)

Judge HUNT: The prisoner will stand up. (Here Miss Anthony arose again.) The sentence of the Court is that you pay a fine of one hundred dollars and the costs of the prosecution.

Miss ANTHONY: May it please your honor, I shall never pay a dollar of your unjust penalty. All the stock in trade I possess is a $10,000 debt, incurred by publishing my paper—The Revolution—four years ago, the sole object of which was to educate all women to do precisely as I have done, rebel against your man-made, unjust, unconstitutional forms of law, that tax, fine, imprison, and hang women, while they deny them the right of representation in the Government; and I shall work on with might and main to pay every dollar of that honest debt, but not a penny shall go to this unjust claim. And I shall earnestly and persistently continue to urge all women to the practical recognition of the old revolutionary maxim, that "Resistance to **tyranny** is obedience to God."

Judge HUNT: Madam, the Court will not order you committed until the fine is paid.

Immediately after the verdict, Miss Anthony, her counsel, her friends, and the jury, passed out together talking over the case. Said Judge Selden: "The war has abolished something besides slavery, it has abolished jury trial. The decision of Justice Hunt was most **iniquitous**. He had as much right to order me hung to the nearest tree, as to take the case from the jury and render the decision he did," and he bowed his head with shame at this **prostitution** of legal power.

Aegis: Shield.
Naturalized: Having become a citizen.
Tyranny: A cruel and unjust government.
Iniquitous: Grossly unjust.
Prostitution: In this case, corruption.

*The jury with freedom now to use their tongues, when too late, also **canvassed** the trial and the injury done. "The verdict of guilty would not have been mine, could I have spoken," said one, "nor should I have been alone. There were others who thought as I did, but we could not speak."*

The decision of Judge Hunt was severely criticised.... Even among those who believed women had no right to vote, and who did not hesitate to say that Miss Anthony's punishment was inadequate, there was a wide questioning as to his legal right to take the case from the jury and enter the verdict of guilty, without permitting them in any way to indicate their opinion. (Stanton et al., pp. 687-89)

What happened next...

By 1875 the Supreme Court ruled that the Fourteenth Amendment did not grant women the right to vote. Anthony spent the rest of her life working for the passage of a federal amendment for women's suffrage. She frequently traveled across the countryside lobbying at state capitals, attending suffrage conventions, meeting with congressmen, and even canvassing door to door. At the last suffrage meeting she attended before she died, Anthony finished her short speech with the encouraging and forceful words, "Failure is impossible." This phrase became a rallying cry among suffragists who nicknamed the federal amendment the "Anthony Amendment." In 1920, 14 years after her death, the Nineteenth Amendment became law. Although Anthony did not live to see her lifelong goal realized, her work made it possible for other women to experience the privileges and rights of full citizenship.

Did you know...

• Anthony was so well known that newspapers nicknamed her "Susan B." and people bought, sold, and traded her autograph much like baseball cards.

Canvassed: Asked people for their opinions.

Susan B. Anthony

Susan B. Anthony (1820-1906) grew up in a large Quaker family in Adams, Massachusetts. There she met many leaders of the antislavery movement who frequently stayed at her family's farm. Anthony began working as a teacher when she was 15 years old, earning $1.50 per week. In addition to abolition, she also actively campaigned for temperance.

Anthony is remembered as one of the key figures in securing women's right to vote. She became leader of the National Woman Suffrage Association (NWSA) in 1869, but when she died in her Rochester, New York, home in 1906 only four states had extended the vote to women. The Nineteenth Amendment —officially granting women suffrage throughout the United States—became law in 1920, 14 years after her death.

- Anthony's numerous letters, diaries, and scrapbooks dating from 1838 to 1900 are housed at the Library of Congress. Her extensive writings provide rich details about an important period in women's history.

- In 1978 the U.S. government minted $1 coins featuring the image of Susan B. Anthony.

For Further Reading

Sherr, Lynn. *Failure Is Impossible: Susan B. Anthony in Her Own Words*. New York: Times Books, 1995.

Stanton, Elizabeth Cady, Susan B. Anthony, and Matilda Joslyn Gage, eds. *History of Woman Suffrage.* Vol. II. Originally published in 1881. Reprinted. New York: Arno Press, 1969.

Weisberg, Barbara. *Susan B. Anthony.* Broomall, Pennsylvania: Chelsea House, 1988.

Home Protection Manual

Written by Frances E. Willard
Published in 1879

Since the 1840s a segment of America's female population has been active in reform societies aimed at outlawing or limiting the use of liquor. This movement, known as temperance, experienced a revival after the Civil War ended in 1865. Alcoholism is said to have been a widespread problem in the developing nation, and reformers once again became interested in eliminating this "evil" beverage.

In 1874 a burst of temperance activity occurred in Hillsboro, Ohio, capturing the attention of newspapers everywhere. Groups of religious women began demonstrating on streetcorners, singing and praying in the name of temperance. The "crusade" spread to other states as more women began to meet and protest outside saloons. Realizing the need for a permanent organization to help ensure their success, female reformers organized the Women's Christian Temperance Union (WCTU) later that same year.

While the two major suffrage organizations were considered radical and even scandalous, temperance was viewed as an appropriate cause for women. Many women in the North and

South joined the WCTU, which quickly became a complex organization of state and local chapters. In 1876 Frances E. Willard, an active union member, began to recommend that women's suffrage was necessary to achieve temperance goals. At first members fiercely opposed Willard's suggestion, but she gradually convinced them that in order to "protect their homes and families" women must be allowed to have a say in decisions concerning the liquor trade in their own communities.

The first so-called "home protection" drive occurred in 1878, when the WCTU collected 180,000 signatures on a petition asking the Illinois state legislature for local, or municipal, suffrage for women. This type of limited suffrage would allow women to vote on local matters only, such as the issuing of liquor licenses to taverns and saloons. Willard, who was a brilliant public speaker, traveled extensively and urged WCTU members to take up the cause of "home protection." In addition to numerous lectures, Willard also published the *Home Protection Manual* in 1879, which served as a guide for local and state temperance unions. The manual contained detailed arguments concerning women's need for the ballot as well as information about forming committees and organizing petition drives addressed to national and state legislatues.

Things to Remember While Reading the *Home Protection Manual:*

- Willard refers to her conversion to temperance during the crusade that swept the nation in 1874. She also mentions the Ribbon Movements, which involved wearing a ribbon badge as a sign of support for temperance.

- Notice how she and others believed that liquor and businesses associated with liquor trade were threatening society. She advocates the concept of "home protection," meaning women should be given the ballot (the right to vote) so they can protect their homes by voting against the liquor interests.

- Some people who opposed women's suffrage felt women already voted in a way—by influencing their sons and husbands. Willard dismisses this popular antisuffrage argument. She rails against the temptation of alcohol and suggests that women would give the temperance movement the number of voters it needed to achieve its goals.

Home Protection, 1879

*Human heads and hearts are much alike. I remember that the great Temperance Crusade of 1874 found me with a beer keg in my cellar, a fatal haziness in my opinions, a **blighting** indifference to the temperance reform upon my will. But how did its intense **pathos** melt my heart; how did its mighty logic tune the lax cords of opinion to concert pitch; how did its miracle of prayer bring thousands to their knees, crying: "Lord, what wouldst thou have me to do?" For myself, I could never be the same after that. As a woman, a patriot, a*

Blighting: Causing to decay.
Pathos: A feeling of pity; sympathy.

Christian, my heart is fixed in deathless **enmity** to all that can intoxicate. The same influences which so transformed one brain and heart are steadily at work to-day in a thousand quiet ways.

The sober second thought of the Woman's Temperance Crusade was organization. The voice of God called to them from the lips of his prophet: "Make a chain, for the land is full of bloody crimes and the city is full of violence." And so in every town and village we are forming these chains of light and of loving helpfulness, which we call "Women's Christian Temperance Unions." We have already twenty-three states organized, with thousands of local auxiliaries. Every day brings fresh **accessions** of women, translated out of the passive and into the active voice on this great question of the protection of their homes. Of the fifty-four thousand papers published in this country eight thousand have temperance facts and figures regularly provided by members of our societies. Temperance literature is being circulated; Our Union, the official **organ** of the Women's National Temperance Society, has a large subscription list; Sabbath-schools are adopting our plans of temperance instruction; and hundreds of juvenile societies are inscribing on their banners: "Tremble, King Alcohol! We shall grow up." Friendly inns and temperance reading rooms are multiplying; Gospel meetings conducted by women are reaching the drinking class in hundreds of communities; the Red and Blue Ribbon Movements have attained magnificent proportions; and all this many-sided work is fast concentrating its influence to place the ballot in the hand of woman, and thus capture for the greatest of reforms old King Majority. Magnificent is the spectacle of these new forces now rallying to the **fray.** Side by side with the 500,000 men whose united energies are expended in making and selling strong drink, we are working day by day. While they brew beer we are brewing public sentiment; while they distill whisky we are distilling facts; while they rectify brandy we are rectifying political constituencies; and ere long their fuming tide of intoxicating liquor

Enmity: Hostility.
Accessions: Additions.
Organ: Publication.
Fray: Fight.

F. Willard

Frances E. Willard

Frances E. Willard (1839-1898) was born and raised in Churchville, New York, then moved to Wisconsin with her family when she was sixteen. After graduating from Northwestern Female College, she began teaching and in 1871 became president of the Evanston College for Ladies in Illinois. Willard resigned from her next post—dean of the Women's College at Northwestern University—in 1874 to become an officer of the Women's Christian Temperance Union (WCTU). She served as its president from 1879 until her death in 1898. Under her leadership the ranks of the WCTU swelled to 250,000 women members, making it one of the most significant political organizations of its time. Willard also helped organize the Prohibition Party in 1882 and a world WCTU organization in 1883 that had 2 million members.

shall be met and driven back by the overwhelming flood of enlightened sentiment and divinely aroused energy....

But, looking deeper, we perceive that, as God has provided in Nature an **antidote** for every poison, and in the kingdom of his grace a compensation for every loss, so in human society he has ordained against King Alcohol, that worst foe of the social state, an enemy beneath whose blows he is to bite the dust. Take the instinct of self-protection (and there is none more deeply seated): What will be its action in woman when the question comes up of licensing the sale of a stimulant which nerves with dangerous strength the arm already so

Antidote: A remedy that counteracts poison.

much stronger than her own, and which at the same time so crazes the brain God meant to guide that manly arm that it strikes down the wife a man loves and the little children for whom when sober he would die? Dependent for the support of herself and little ones and for the maintenance of her home, upon the strength which alcohol masters and the skill it renders **futile,** *will the wife and mother cast her vote to open or to close the rum-shop door over against that home?*

Then there is a second instinct, so much higher and more sacred that I would not speak of it too near the first. It is as deep, but how high it reaches up toward Heaven—the instinct of a mother's love, a wife's devotion, a sister's faithfulness, a daughter's loyalty! Friends, this love of women's hearts was given for purposes of wider blessing to poor humanity than some of us have dreamed. Before this century shall [end,] the rays of love which shine out from woman's heart shall no longer be, as now, divergent so far as the liquor traffic is concerned; but through that magic lens, that powerful sunglass which we term the ballot, they shall converge their power, and burn and blaze on the saloon, till it shrivels up and in **lurid** *vapors curls away like mist under the hot gaze of sunshine. Ere long our brothers, hedged about by temptations, even as we are by safeguards, shall thus match force with force; shall set over against the dealer's* **avarice** *our timid instinct of self-protection, and match the drinker's love of liquor by our love of him. When this is done you will have doomed the rum power in America, even as you doomed the slave power when you gave the ballot to the slave.*

"But women should content themselves with educating public sentiment," say one. Nay, we can shorten the process…. Let the great guns of influence, not pointing into vacancy, be swung to the level of **benignant** *use and pointed on election day straight into the faces of the foe! "No; but she should train her son to vote aright," suggests another. But if she could go along with him, and thus make one vote two, should we then have a* **superfluous** *majority in a struggle intense as this one is to be? And then*

Futile: Useless.
Lurid: Gruesome; shocking.
Avarice: Greed.
Benignant: Beneficial.
Superfluous: Extra.

F. Willard

*how unequal is her combat for the right to train her boy! Enter yonder saloon. See them gathered around their fiery or their foamy cups.... What are they talking of, those sovereign citizens? The times have changed. It is no longer tariff or no tariff, resumption of **specie** payments, or even the behavior of our Southern brethren that occupies their thought. No. Home questions have come elbowing their way to the front. The child in the midst is also in the marketplace, and they are bidding for him there, the politicians of the saloon. So skillfully will they make out the slate, so vigorously turn the crank of the machine, that, in spite of churches and temperance societies combined, the measures dear to them will triumph and measures dear to the fond mother heart will fail. Give her, at least, a fair chance to offset by her ballot the **machinations** which imperil her son....*

*During the past years the women who pioneered the equal suffrage movement, and whose perceptions of justice were keen as a **Damascus** blade, took for their rallying cry: "Taxation without representation is tyranny." But the average woman, who has nothing to be taxed, declines to go forth to battle on that issue. Since the Crusade, plain, practical temperance people have begun appealing to this same average woman, saying "With your vote we can close the saloons that tempt your boys to ruin"; and behold! they have transfixed with the arrow of conviction that mother's heart, and she is ready for the fray. Not rights, but duties; not her need alone, but that of her children and her country; not the "woman," but the "human" question is stirring women's hearts and breaking down their prejudice today. For they begin to perceive the divine fact that civilization, in proportion as it becomes Christianized, will make increasing demands upon creation's gentler half; that the Ten Commandments and the Sermon on the Mount are voted up or voted down upon election day; and that a military **exigency** requires the army of the Prince of Peace to call out its reserves...*

Friends, there is always a way out for humanity. Evermore in earth's affairs God works by means. To-day he hurls

Specie: Coin.
Machinations: Evil plotting.
Damascus: Early type of steel.
Exigency: Urgency.

back upon us our complaining cry: "How long? O Lord! how long?" Even as he answered faint-hearted Israel, so he replies to us: "What can I do for this people that I have not done? Speak unto the children of Israel that they go forward."

> There's a light about to beam,
> There's a **fount** about to stream,
> There's a warmth about to glow,
> There's a flower about to blow,
> There's a midnight blackness
> Changing into gray;
> Men of thoughts, of votes, of action,
> Clear the way!
> Aid that dawning tongue and pen;
> Aid it, hopes of honest men;
> Aid it, for the hour is ripe,
> And our earnest must not slacken into play.
> Men of thoughts of votes of action,
> Clear the way!
> (Willard in Leeman, pp. 122-36)

What happened next...

Frances Willard became president of the WCTU in 1879. Under her leadership it became the largest and most powerful women's organization of the century with 250,000 members. Historians are unsure about whether Willard's work helped or harmed women's suffrage. Unfortunately, by linking temperance to suffrage, suffrage became an easy target for the wealthy and powerful liquor lobbies to attack. In fact, some leaders of the women's movement believe suffrage was delayed or denied in several state campaigns because of the liquor interests. However, Willard can be credited with providing new energy to a fractured and failing suffrage movement. Her ability to orga-

Fount: Fountain.

nize and to persuade certainly made a lasting impression on the temperance and women's movements.

Did you know...

- During the bicycling craze of the 1890s Willard, like many women, learned to enjoy the exercise, independence, and transportation provided by the bicycle. In 1895 she published a bestselling book about her experiences called *A Wheel within a Wheel: How I Learned to Ride the Bicycle, with Some Reflections by the Way.*

- A statue of Willard sits in the rotunda of the Capitol in Washington, D.C., with the dedication: "The first woman of the 19th century, the most beloved character of her times."

- The Eighteenth Amendment, or Prohibition Amendment, was ratified (approved) in 1919; it banned the manufacture, transportation, and sale of alcoholic beverages. The Nineteenth Amendment, or Women's Suffrage Amendment, was ratified one year later.

For Further Reading

Bordin, Ruth. *Frances Willard: A Biography.* Chapel Hill: University of North Carolina Press, 1986.

Leeman, Richard W. *"Do Everything" Reform: The Oratory of Frances E. Willard.* New York: Greenwood Press, 1992.

Papachristou, Judith. *Women Together.* New York: Alfred A. Knopf, 1976.

Reminiscences, 1819–1899

Selections from an original text
Written by Julia Ward Howe
Published in 1899

The Industrial Revolution—a period of rapid economic growth and mechanical advancement that began in England at the end of the eighteenth century—changed the way people lived and worked in the United States after the Civil War. Train tracks began to crisscross the nation, factories and cities sprang up throughout the country, and for the first time homes were filled with the glow of gaslight instead of candlelight. This great era of invention touched the lives of all Americans from farmers to newly arrived immigrants to factory workers. Innovations also changed the ways women—then the sole workers on the domestic front—took care of their families and households. Advances such as indoor plumbing and the sewing machine gave women more free time, thus allowing them to pursue interests outside of the home.

From the late 1870s to the 1920s millions of American women joined social clubs. These clubs were different from the earlier all-female societies devoted to causes such as antislavery

National Woman Suffrage Association

Founded in May, 1869

American Woman Suffrage Association

Founded in November, 1869

The leaders involved with the abolitionist (antislavery) and women's rights movements finally and formally split in 1869 over their differing opinions concerning the Fifteenth Amendment, which granted voting rights to black men but not to women. Elizabeth Cady Stanton and Susan B. Anthony believed it was time to focus solely on women's rights and founded the National Woman Suffrage Association (NWSA) in May 1869. At first they thought only women should be admitted as members; they felt that male abolitionists had harmed their cause by placing the rights of black men above the rights of women of all colors. The NSWA's fight for suffrage was directed at the federal level.

Later in 1869 Lucy Stone, Julia Ward Howe, and other prominent female leaders organized the American Woman Suffrage Association (AWSA), a less controversial organization than the NWSA. The AWSA welcomed men as members and as leaders in the struggle for women's suffrage. The suffrage activities of the AWSA took place at the state level. The two associations coexisted for more than 20 years, reflecting different styles of political leadership. Finally in 1890 the organizations combined their efforts with the creation of the National American Woman Suffrage Association.

and women's suffrage (meaning the right to vote). Women in the North and South, in towns and in rural communities, who were interested in self-improvement formed numerous clubs based on common interests. While some clubs were short-lived, others, like the New England Woman's Club prospered for many years. As the number and size of women's clubs continued to grow, a national network called the General Federation of Women's Clubs formed in 1890.

The New England Woman's Club, organized in 1868 by Julia Ward Howe and other Boston women, attracted intellectuals, people who enjoy pondering and discussing the meaning of books, plays, and philosophical theories. The club's goal was to "furnish a quiet central resting-place and place of meeting in Boston, for the comfort and convenience of its members" and to be "an organized social center for united thought and action." The New England Woman's Club enjoyed a great deal of success for many decades and actually achieved a degree of political and social power in Boston.

Howe also helped organize the New England Woman Suffrage Association in 1868 and the American Woman Suffrage Association (AWSA) in 1869. As one of America's favorite patriots, she gave much needed credibility to the women's rights movement. During Civil War she had written *The Battle Hymn of the Republic,* which became the most popular war song of the Union forces. After the war she became increasingly involved with the women's clubs and women's suffrage movements. She wrote about her life's experiences in the autobiographical book *Reminiscences, 1819-1899* in 1899.

Things to Remember While Reading
Reminiscences, 1819-1899:

- Howe mentions she was reluctant at first about joining a women's club. She also tried to avoid sitting on the speaker's platform when she attended a suffrage meeting. Like many women of her time, she feared being associated with anything controversial.

- Originally opposed to suffrage, Howe changed her opinion about women's rights. She began to understand the vast array of reasons why women should be allowed to vote.

- Howe writes about learning the fine art of public speaking and the running of large meetings. She traveled extensively throughout New England delivering lectures in support of women's suffrage.

- By giving so much of herself in terms of time and hard work, Howe received many rewards in return. She truly enjoyed meeting different people in her travels and received great satisfaction from helping others.

Reminiscences, 1819–1899

I sometimes feel as if words could not express the comfort and instruction which have come to me in the later years of my life from two sources. One of these has been the better acquaintance with my own sex; the other, the experience of the power resulting from associated action in behalf of worthy objects.

*During the first two thirds of my life I looked to the masculine ideal of character as the only true one. I sought its inspiration, and referred my merits and demerits to its judicial verdict. In an unexpected hour a new light came to me, showing me a world of thought and of character quite beyond the limits within which I had hitherto been content to abide. The new domain now made clear to me was that of true womanhood, —woman no longer in her **ancillary** relation to her opposite, man, but in her direct relation to the divine plan and purpose, as a free agent, fully sharing with man every human right and every human responsibility. This discovery was like the addition of a new continent to the map of the world, or of a new testament to the old ordinances….*

It did not come to me all at once. In my attempts at philosophizing I at length reached the conclusion that woman must be the moral and spiritual equivalent of man. How, otherwise, could she be entrusted with the awful and inevitable responsibilities of maternity?…

*While my mind was engaged with these questions, the civil war came to an end, leaving the slave not only **emancipated,** but endowed with the full dignity of citizenship. The women of the North had greatly helped to open the door which admitted him to freedom and its safeguard, the ballot. Was this door to be shut in their face?*

Ancillary: *Subordinate.*
Emancipated: *Freed.*

Susan B. Anthony helped form the NWSA, a suffrage organization that rivaled Howe's more conservative AWSA.

While I followed, rather unwillingly, this train of thought, an invitation was sent me to attend a parlor meeting to be held with the view of forming a woman's club in Boston. I presented myself at this meeting, and gave a **languid** assent to the measures proposed. These were to hire a parlor or parlors in some convenient locality, and to furnish and keep them open for the convenience of ladies residing in the city and its suburbs. Out of this small and modest beginning was gradually developed the plan of the New England Woman's Club, a strong and stately association destined, I believe, to last for many years, and leaving behind it, at this time of my writing, a record of three decades of happy and acceptable service.

While our club life was still in its beginning, I was invited and induced to attend a meeting in behalf of woman suffrage. Indeed, I had given my name to the call for this meeting, relying upon the assurance given me by Colonel Thomas Wentworth Higginson [a Unitarian minister involved in the antislavery and women's movements], that it would be conducted in a very liberal and friendly spirit, without bitterness or extravagance. The place appointed was Horticultural Hall. The morning was **inclement;** and as I strayed into the hall in my rainy-day suit, nothing was further from my mind than the thought that I should take any part in the day's proceedings.

I had hoped not to be noticed by the officers of the meeting, and was rather disconcerted when a message reached me requesting me to come up and take a seat on the platform. This I did very reluctantly. I was now face to face with a new order of things. Here, indeed, were some whom I had long known and honored: [William Lloyd] Garrison, Wendell Phillips, Colonel Higginson, and my dear pastor, James Freeman

Clarke. But here was also Lucy Stone [a suffragist and lecturer for women's rights, perhaps most famous for retaining her maiden name as a protest against unequitable marital laws], who had long been the object of one of my imaginary dislikes. As I looked into her sweet, womanly face and heard her earnest voice, I felt that the object of my distaste had been a mere phantom, conjured up by silly and senseless misrepresentations. Here stood the true woman, pure, noble, great-hearted, with the light of her good life shining in every feature of her face. Here, too, I saw the husband whose devotion so ably seconded her life-work.

The arguments to which I now listened were simple, strong, and convincing. These champions, who had fought so long and so **valiantly** for the slave, now turned the search-light of their intelligence upon the condition of woman, and demanded for the mothers of the community the civil rights which had recently been accorded to the negro. They asked for nothing more and nothing less than the administration of that impartial justice for which, if for anything, a Republican government should stand.

When they requested me to speak, which they did presently, I could only say, "I am with you." I have been with them ever since, and have never seen any reason to go back from the pledge then given. Strangely, as it then seemed to me, the arguments which I had stored up in my mind against the political enfranchisement of women were really so many reasons in its favor. All that I had felt regarding the sacredness and importance of the woman's part in private life now appeared to me equally applicable to the part which she should bear in public life....

In the little band of workers which I had joined, I was soon called upon to perform **yeoman's** service. I was expected to attend meetings and to address audiences, at first in the neighborhood of Boston, afterwards in many remote places, Cleveland, Chicago, St. Louis. Among those who led or followed the new movement, I naturally encountered some indi-

Valiantly: Courageously.
Yeoman: Hard worker; farmer.

Julia Ward Howe

Julia Ward Howe (1819-1910), the daughter of a successful banker, was born in New York City. She received an excellent private education, learning to read Greek, Latin, and the works of German philosopher Emmanuel Kant. Howe helped her husband, Samuel Greatly Howe, edit the famous antislavery newspaper *The Commonwealth*. She wrote *The Battle Hymn of the Republic* in 1861. In addition to being an honored lay preacher, she was a popular lecturer and author of biographies, drama, travel books, verse, and children's songs. In 1908 she became the first woman elected to the American Academy of Arts and Letters.

viduals in whom vanity and personal ambition were conspicuous. But I found mostly among my new associates a great heart of religious conviction and a genuine spirit of self-sacrifice.

My own contributions to the work appeared to me less valuable than I had hoped to find them. I had at first everything to learn with regard to public speaking, and Lucy Stone and Mrs. [Mary A.] Livermore [a reformer and publisher also involved in the temperance movement] were much more at home on the platform than I was. I was called upon to preside over conventions, having never learned the rules of debate. I was obliged to address large audiences, having been accustomed to use my voice only in parlors. Gradually all this bettered itself. I became familiar with the order of proceedings, and learned to modulate my voice. More important even than these things, I learned something of the range of popular sympathies, and of the power of **apprehension** to be found in average audiences. All of these experiences, the failures, the effort, and the final achievement, were most useful to me.

In years that followed I gave what I could to the cause, but all that I gave was repaid to me a thousandfold. I had always had to do with women of character and intelligence, but I found in my new friends a clearness of insight, a strength and steadfastness of purpose, which enabled them to take a position of command, in view of the questions of the hour....

The novelty of the topic in the mind of the general public [women's suffrage] brought together large audiences in Boston and in the neighboring towns. Lucy Stone's **fervent** zeal, always guided by her faultless feeling of **propriety**, the earnest pleading of her husband, the brilliant **eloquence** and personal magnetism of Mary A. Livermore,—all these things combined to give to our platform a novel and sustained attraction. Noble men, aye, the noblest, stood with us in our endeavor, —some, like Senator Hoar and George S. Hale, to explain and illustrate the logical sequence which should lead to the recognition of our citizenship; others, like Wendell Phillips, George William Curtis, and Henry Ward Beecher [a clergyman noted for his powerful speaking ability; supporter of women's suffrage and brother of teacher Catherine Beecher and author Harriet Beecher Stowe] able to overwhelm the crumbling defenses of the old order with the storm and flash of their eloquence.

We acted, one and all, under the powerful stimulus of hope. The object which we labored to accomplish was so legitimate and rational, so directly in the line of our religious belief, of our political institutions, that it appeared as if we had only to unfold our new banner, bright with the **blazon** of applied Christianity, and march on to victory. The black man had received the vote. Should the white woman be less considered than he?

During the recent war the women of our country had been as ministering angels to our armies, forsaking homes of

Apprehension: *Perception.*
Fervent: *Showing great emotion.*
Propriety: *Social acceptability.*
Eloquence: *Persuasive speaking.*
Blazon: *Fancy seal or emblem, like a coat of arms.*

*ease and luxury to bring **succor** and comfort to the camp-hospital and battlefield. Those who tarried at home had labored incessantly to supply the needs of those at the front. Should they not be counted among the citizens of the great Republic? Moreover, we women had year after year worked to build, maintain, and fill the churches throughout the land.... Surely we should be invited to pass in with our brothers to the larger liberty now shown to be our just due.*

We often spoke in country towns, where our morning meetings could be but poorly attended, for the reason that the women of the place were busy with the preparation of the noonday meal. Our evening sessions in such places were precious to school-teachers and factory hands.

*Ministers opened to us their churches, and the women of their congregations worked together to provide for us places of refreshment and **repose.** We met the real people face to face and hand to hand. It was a period of awakened thought, of quickened and enlarged sympathy.*

(Howe, pp. 272-79)

What happened next...

Howe provided valuable prestige and respectability to the women's suffrage movement. The AWSA, which she helped organize, acted far more conservatively than its rival, the National Woman Suffrage Association (NWSA). (The NWSA, led by Susan B. Anthony and Elizabeth Cady Stanton, frequently created controversy by working for issues such as divorce reform.) After a 20-year long split, the two groups united, forming the National American Woman Suffrage Association in 1890.

Howe's song *The Battle Hymn of the Republic* has a special place in American history. Originally written in 1861 to help free slaves, it became the anthem of the women's suffrage movement in the 1910s and the civil rights movement in the 1960s. It

Succor: Help in a time of need.

Repose: Rest.

was also played as Senator Robert Kennedy's funeral train carried his body from New York to Washington, D.C., in 1968.

Did you know...

• Howe is also credited with introducing the idea for Mother's Day. Her husband, Samuel Greatly Howe, is remembered for his contributions as a teacher and director of the prestigious Perkins School for the Blind.

• When Charles Dickens, the famous English author, attended a dinner at the New York Press Club in 1868, women journalists were not allowed to participate. This event prompted a female journalist, Jennie C. Croly, to organize one of the first women's clubs, *Sorosis*.

• One of the early biographies written about Howe won a Pulitzer Prize, an award recognizing significant accomplishments in journalism, literature, and music. The award-winning book *Julia Ward Howe, 1819-1910* was written by Laura E. Richards and M. H. Elliot in 1915.

For Further Reading

Clifford, Deborah P. *Mine Eyes Have Seen the Glory: A Biography of Julia Ward Howe.* Boston: Little, Brown, 1979.

Howe, Julia Ward. *Reminiscences, 1819-1899.* Boston: Houghton, Mifflin, 1899.

Papachristou, Judith. *Women Together.* New York: Alfred A. Knopf, 1976.

Do You Know?

Written by Carrie Chapman Catt
Delivered c. 1912

Fifty years after the first women's right convention, which took place in Seneca Falls, New York, in 1848, women continued to fight for the right to vote. The last living founder of the movement, Susan B. Anthony, resigned as president of the major suffrage organization, the National American Woman Suffrage Association (NWSA), in 1900. The eighty-year-old Anthony had devoted her life to the suffrage cause, traveling back and forth across the country, giving lectures at conventions, and organizing petition drives. She faced an awesome task in choosing her successor, for the future of women's suffrage depended on a strong, effective national leader. Anthony appointed Carrie Chapman Catt, an experienced and talented suffrage worker who had already organized suffrage campaigns in several states.

Anthony chose Catt because of her remarkable talents at organizing large campaign drives involving multiple locations. Catt had staged successful suffrage campaigns in Colorado (1893) and Idaho (1896) and unsuccessful campaigns in California (1896) and Iowa (1897). During her first term as president of NAWSA

(1900-1904), she and other suffrage leaders continued to focus their efforts on individual state campaigns. Frustrated and worn out from several exhausting state referendum defeats, Catt resigned as president in 1904 to care for her ill husband.

After the devastating loss of her husband Catt eventually regained her energies. She became involved with the international women's suffrage movement, serving as president of the

Nineteenth Amendment

Proposed in June, 1919
Ratified in August, 1920

Women's rights leader Susan B. Anthony convinced Senator S. C. Pomeroy of Kansas to introduce the first federal women's suffrage amendment to Congress in 1868. Unfortunately, the proposed amendment failed that year—and every year it was reintroduced between 1868 and 1896. Women fought for the right to vote for two generations before finally achieving it. The bill allowing women the right to vote passed Congress in 1919 and was ratified by the states in 1920. The simple wording of the Nineteenth Amendment does not reveal the tremendous effort of its original proponents, nor the monumental impact it had on American society.

AMENDMENT XIX

Section 1. The right of citizens of the United States to vote shall not be denied or abridged by the United States or by any State on account of sex.

International Woman Suffrage Alliance from 1904 to 1923. Catt traveled to Europe several times, meeting with women suffrage leaders worldwide. Her work as an international leader is said to have given considerable leverage to the suffrage movement in the United States. Meanwhile, NAWSA was almost at a standstill under the direction and leadership of Anna Howard Shaw, who had taken over as president when Catt resigned back in 1904.

Under considerable pressure from fellow suffrage workers, Catt reluctantly became the leader of NAWSA again, serving as its final president from 1915 to 1920. Catt helped lead the suffrage movement over the finish line with the passage of the Nineteenth Amendment in 1920, which granted women the right to vote.

Things to Remember While Reading *Do You Know?*:

• Catt was very involved with international suffrage and makes several references to the voting status of women in other countries.

- In spite of advancements in education and employment early in the twentieth century, American women were still denied the right to vote. Catt points out the contradictions of a society that educates women and allows them to be wage earners yet refuses to grant them suffrage.

- Proponents of women's suffrage imply that women—supposedly being more moral than men—would make more moral voters. They argue the world would be a better place if women voted.

- Pro-suffrage workers referred to the popular rallying cry of the American Revolution: "No taxation without representation." Catt points out that it is unfair for women to pay taxes on their wages and on property but not vote as citizens to decide the use of public funds.

Do You Know?

DO YOU KNOW what woman suffrage means? and do you know that the question of the right of women to self-government is one which is commanding the attention of the whole civilized world? That working woman suffrage organizations of representative men and women exist in twenty-one countries: Australia, Austria, Belgium, Bohemia, Bulgaria, Canada, Denmark, Finland, France, Germany, Great Britain, Italy, Iceland, Holland, Hungary, Norway, Russia, South Africa, Sweden, Switzerland, United States? This is true, and the status of woman suffrage in many Nations, which are not ordinarily considered by Americans as so progressive as our own, demands that every voter in the United States, as well as every woman, should give intelligent and conscientious examination into the merits of the question....

DO YOU KNOW that the report of the Commissioner of Education for 1907 states that ... a much larger number of girls than boys receive the higher education offered by the *public schools.... Do you know that if men and women had been equally entitled to the **franchise** in 1900, there would have been 20,000 fewer **illiterates** among the women than men, who between the ages of 21 and 24 would have cast their first presidential vote?*

*   **DO YOU KNOW** that if the same conditions relative to education shall continue for the next twenty years, and women still remain disfranchised, we shall witness the curious spectacle of the more illiterate sex making laws for the less illiterate sex?*

*   **DO YOU KNOW** that women will add a distinct moral element to the present vote? Is it not true that in every State, the per cent. of women in the penitentiaries and police courts is extremely small as compared to the number of men criminals? Is it not well known that women constitute a minority of drunkards, gamblers, thieves, counterfeiters, etc.? Is it not true that for every prostitute there are at least two men responsible for her immorality? Is it not true that in every immoral institution, and in every factor which tends to handicap the moral progress of society, women are in the minority? Is it not true that in the churches, and in all **altruistic** and moral movements whose chief motive is the uplifting of humanity, women are in the majority? Why, then, should their votes be feared? Senator Warren, of Wyoming, sums it up when he says: "Wyoming women nearly all vote, and since in Wyoming, as elsewhere, the majority of women are good and not bad, the result is good and not evil."...*

*   **DO YOU KNOW** that there is a steady increase in the per cent. of women wage earners and women in business? In 1880 the women engaged in gainful occupation were 14.7 per cent. of the total; in 1890, 17 per cent.; in 1900, 18.8 per cent....*

*   **DO YOU KNOW** why men are voters—by what guarantee they hold their right to the ballot? A citizen's right to share in government was theirs by inheritance. Who secured it? What was the plea that won this privilege? If you wish to go back to the very beginning of modern democracy, we*

Franchise: The right to vote.
Illiterates: People unable to read or write.
Altruistic: Showing concern for others.

140   Catt

Carrie Chapman Catt

Carrie Chapman Catt (1859-1947) was born in Ripon, Wisconsin, raised in Iowa, and attended Iowa State College. After working as a teacher, Catt became a high school principle and, later, one of the first woman superintendents of schools in Iowa. She was active in women's clubs, wrote a women's newspaper column, and organized the Iowa Woman Suffrage Association in 1887. Catt served two terms as president of the National American Woman Suffrage Association (NAWSA)—from 1900 to 1904 and 1915 to 1920. After helping to form the League of Women Voters, she immersed herself in the peace movement of the 1920s, supporting both the League of Nations and the United Nations.

shall find it when the barons of England, holding vast estates, and furnishing the wealth that supported English wars, demanded of King John a share in his power, and enforced their demand with the ultimatum: "No division of power, no more taxes from our estates." The king yielded, and the **Magna Charta** was written....

DO YOU KNOW that in the colonies only taxpayers were voters; that many additional restrictions were put upon voters, such as nativity, moral and religious qualifications? Then came the great Revolution with its war cry "Taxation without representation is **tyranny**." Yet few, if any, applied this **axiom** to individuals. It was the claim of a colony against a mother country....

Magna Charta: English charter of rights dated 1215, designed to ensure that kings ruled justly.

Tyranny: A cruel and unjust act of government.

Axiom: Established principle.

DO YOU KNOW that later [after the American Revolution] a great movement inspired by the broad views of human liberty, held by American statesmen in the early days of government, arose, which in time removed the property qualifications? "Government," said they, should "derive their just powers from the consent of the governed."... Yet it was a hundred years from the date when the first original State removed tax qualification before the last one did, so reluctant is power to divide its authority.

DO YOU KNOW that even yet there was no republic, but instead an aristocracy of color sprang up into the place of the aristocracy of property, and white men ruled black men, even though free? Later when all black men were **emancipated**, broad-minded white men said: "Give the black man a chance. The ballot is the only peaceable means of defense, give it to him." And it was done.... Do you know, throughout this century of change, that no argument for the extension of the suffrage to men was ever made except "Taxation without representation is tyranny," and "Governments derive their just powers from the consent of the governed?" The unanswerable logic of these two principles is the guarantee by which all men hold their ballots. You are a voter today because your predecessors in the history of the world were willing to divide their governmental authority with you. Brother, will you not remember the Golden Rule, and now do by others as others have done by you?

DO YOU KNOW why women were not included among voters when the government was based upon taxation? Because they were not taxpayers. When a woman married (and there were few unmarried women in those days) all her belongings passed to her husband's possession, and therefore he was recognized as the taxpayers, and often secured the right to a vote upon her property. Nor could a married woman accumulate property; for she was not permitted to control her own wages, nor to go into business on her own account.... When a woman married, she became legally dead. As [Sir

Emancipated: Freed from slavery.

William] Blackstone [famous eighteenth-century English jurist] put it, "Husband and wife were one, and that one, the husband." No wonder our statesmen did not include these women, who had no legal existence, among the voters.

DO YOU KNOW that these conditions no longer exist, and that a husband and wife are now two? Married women may now own property. The law no longer recognizes them as the servants of their husbands, but as their equals. What is taxation? The confiscation of private property for public purposes. Who confiscates it? Voters. Is not an opportunity to consent or refuse a just part of such procedure? Is there any reason why the taxation of the non-voter has suddenly become justifiable? Is it not as much tyranny today as in any other period of American history? Do you say such taxation is fair because some women taxpayers are satisfied to have it so? Is it right to continue a wrong because the persons wronged make small protest?...

DO YOU KNOW that many women are as earnestly anxious to vote as any man in the land? Should not all men and women who are public-spirited and liberty-loving have the privilege of the ballot?... The movement to divide official power has always come from those who possessed it, and never through the appeal of the disfranchised. Woman suffrage, like man suffrage, must come through the generous action of those who now possess the power to give it. In fact, more women ... have asked for the ballot than have men of any disfranchised class in the history of the world.

DO YOU KNOW that, while women are ruled out, the highest intelligence and morality will never be fully represented in any community in its law, since intelligence and morality must always be averaged at the ballot-box with ignorance and immorality? It is plain that wherever intelligence and morality **predominate** over ignorance and immorality the trend of civilization must be upward, and since women can offer a higher per cent. of morality, and certainly an equal

Predominate: Having greater power.

amount of intelligence with men, it requires no demonstration to show that women will help make the world better.

DO YOU KNOW that in no State where the people have extended the suffrage to women ... has there been any effort to repeal such laws? There are people in the States where women vote who were anti-suffragists before women were enfranchised, and who are so still, but every year the number of those who advocate woman suffrage is larger than the year before. Hundreds of the most representative people, both men and women, have testified time and again in print ... that woman suffrage has brought none of the evils which the opponents fear, but instead has brought much positive good. It has enlarged the outlook of women, increased their intelligence and self-reliance, has rendered homes happier because of more intellectual companionship, has ennobled men and dignified politics. In all the places where women vote, the opponents, thus far, have not found a dozen respectable men who assert over their own names and addresses that it has had any bad results.... Do you know any logical, sound reason why the intelligence and individuality of women should not entitle them to the rights and the privileges of self-government? (Catt, pp. 1-15)

What happened next...

Historians credit Catt with helping to secure the passage of the Nineteenth Amendment. As president of NAWSA she devised a "Winning Plan" in 1916, which outlined responsibilities for suffrage organizations within all states. By coordinating efforts at both the state and national levels, Catt succeeded in lobbying Congress as well as state legislatures. When ratification of the Nineteenth Amendment appeared certain in 1920, Catt helped reorganize the 2 million members of NAWSA into the League of

Women Voters (LWV). This new organization helped teach women an understanding of public affairs and continued its activities at the dawn of the twenty-first century. In 1920, Catt gave women advice about their new right to vote by noting: "The vote of yours has cost millions of dollars and the lives of thousands of women.... Prize it.... Understand what it means and what it can do for your country.... Progress is calling on you to make no pause. Act."

Did you know...

- Catt was an ardent pacifist, a person who opposed war. In 1925 she helped start the National Committee on the Cause and Cure of War, the largest women's peace group of the '20s.

- She and her husband, George W. Catt, had a prenuptial contract (a legal agreement regarding the terms of their marriage). This agreement allowed Catt to devote at least four months of each year to women's suffrage activities.

- Catt's parents believed a college education for their daughter was unnecessary since she would no doubt be a married woman one day. But Carrie Chapman Catt disagreed; she paid her own way through college by working as a schoolteacher.

For Further Reading

Catt, Carrie Chapman. *Do You Know?* Originally published c. 1912. Microfilmed from an original housed in the State Historical Society of Wisconsin.

Flexner, Eleanor. *Century of Struggle: The Woman's Rights Movement in the United States.* Revised edition. Cambridge, Massachusetts: Belknap/Harvard University Press, 1975.

Crusade for Justice

Selections from the autobiography of Ida B. Wells-Barnett
Published in 1970

Between 1890 and 1920 women across America began forming numerous clubs and organizations. The women's club movement spread throughout the northern and southern states as well as the western territories and included both black and white women. In addition to providing members with companionship, encouragement, and a sense of empowerment, these clubs sought to bring about social change. Both black and white women's clubs frequently became involved with the struggle for women's suffrage (the right to vote). Ida B. Wells-Barnett, a former journalist and teacher, helped organize black women's clubs in several cities. She also started what is thought to have been the first black women's suffrage club, located in Chicago.

Wells-Barnett was already a national figure when she became active in the women's club movement. She helped lead a national crusade against lynching, a horrific practice of racially motivated murder that reached alarming proportions in the post-Reconstruction era of the 1880s and 1890s. Her four-decade-

long crusade against lynching began in 1892, when one of her close friends was killed in Natchez, Mississippi, by white extremists. Wells-Barnett experienced firsthand the outrage and injustice associated with racist crimes. She became a target of violence herself when her writings and lectures began to win public support. Her many years of working to improve conditions for African Americans made Wells-Barnett realize the importance of voting rights for black women.

In 1913 women suffragists began an active campaign for women's right to vote—at least in presidential elections—in Wells-Barnett's home state of Illinois. While not an ideal goal, restricted suffrage represented a step toward political equality for the women of Illinois. Wells-Barnett recognized the importance of the campaign and helped organize a black women's suffrage organization called the Alpha Suffrage Club. Working separately—but toward one goal—black and white suffragists successfully convinced the state legislators to grant presidential suffrage to Illinois women in 1913.

Suffragists march up New York City's Fifth Avenue in 1913.

Wells-Barnett also helped raise the issue of racial integration in the national suffrage movement. She traveled to Washington, D.C., to participate in a major suffrage parade honoring Woodrow Wilson's inauguration as president. Planning to march with her fellow delegates from Chicago, Wells-Barnett refused to form a "colored delegation" at the rear of the parade. She eventually joined the multiracial Chicago delegation, escorted by white supporters.

Wells-Barnett began to write about her life's accomplishments in an autobiography, but she died before its completion. Her eldest daughter, Alfreda M. Duster, completed the manuscript; the finished text, *Crusade for Justice,* was published in 1970, nearly 40 years after her mother's death.

Things to Remember While Reading *Crusade for Justice*:

- Wells-Barnett recognizes the political power of a "voting bloc" and tries to organize the black community in support of a particular candidate.

- Frustrated with politicians who ignored their black constituents, she attempts to work with candidates who promise to help the black community after election.

- Notice the practice of "buying votes." Corrupt politicians in Chicago and other cities would pay people to vote a certain way in an election.

Crusade for Justice

It was about this time [1913] that the Illinois legislature was considering the question of enfranchising the women voters of the state. I had been a member of the Women's Suffrage Association all during my residence in Illinois, but somehow I had not been able to get very much interest among our club women.

When I saw that we were likely to have a restricted suffrage, and the white women of the organization were working like beavers to bring it about, I made another effort to get our women interested.

With the assistance of one or two of my suffrage friends, I organized what afterward became known as the Alpha Suffrage Club. The women who joined were extremely interested when I showed them that we could use our vote for the advantage of ourselves and our race. We organized the **block** system, and once a week we met to report progress. The women at first were very much discouraged.

They said that the men jeered at them and told them they ought to be at home taking care of the babies. Others insisted that the women were trying to take the place of men and wear the trousers. I urged each one of the workers to go back and tell the women that we wanted them to register so that they could help put a colored man in the city council.

This line of argument appealed very strongly to them, since we had already taken part in several campaigns where men had run independent for **alderman**.

The work of these women was so effective that when registration day came, the Second **Ward** was the sixth highest of the thirty-five wards of the city.

Our men politicians were surprised because not one of them, not even our ministers, had said one word to influence women to take advantage of the suffrage opportunity Illinois had given to her daughters. At the next primary campaign for alderman, because of the women's vote, Mr. W. R. Cowan, who was running independently, came within 167 votes of beating the ward organization candidate, Mr. Hugh Norris.

This happened on Tuesday. When the Alpha Suffrage Club convened for its regular meeting Wednesday night, we found present Mr. Samuel Ettelson and Mr. Oscar DePriest. These gentlemen came representing the ward organization.... [They] told us how much they admired the splendid work that had been done by us and assured us that if we would turn in and give our support to the organization candidate, who had won by only 167 votes the day before, the organization, hav-

Block: *Group united by a common interest.*

Alderman: *Member of a city legislative (lawmaking) body.*

Ward: *A division of a city for electoral purposes.*

Ida B. Wells-Barnett

Ida B. Wells-Barnett (1862-1931), the eldest of eight children, was born into slavery in Mississippi just six months before the passage of the Emancipation Proclamation (which freed slaves in rebelling states during the Civil War). She attended Shaw University, and at the age of sixteen—following the tragic deaths of her parents in a yellow fever epidemic —she started working as a teacher to support her brothers and sisters. After moving to Memphis, Tennessee, in 1883 she began her career as a journalist, writing for numerous black publications throughout the South. Wells-Barnett received many threats because of her antilynching writings, forcing her to leave the South and relocate to New York City. She married Ferdinand L. Barnett, a lawyer, in 1895, and together they raised a family in the Chicago area.

ing realized that there was now a demand for a colored man, would itself nominate one at the next vacancy....

The women ... wanted to know when there would be another vacancy.... Another question was asked—How could we be sure that the organization would keep its promise as made by Mr. DePriest?...

After a most interesting session the gentlemen withdrew and the club proceeded to act on their suggestions. We sent out letters to representative organizations.... Most of them ridiculed the idea that the organization meant to do any such thing as suggested and thought we were wasting our time.

In due course of time Mr. Harding was elected state senator which, of course, did make his position as alderman vacant. The very next day after the November election, Mr. Oscar DePriest called together a group of colored men to a dinner, and informed them that he had already received the endorsement of the Second Ward organization for Mr. Harding's place until the following February and election in April.

For that entire eight months Mr. DePriest interviewed every person of any influence, ringing doorbells and asking their support. Of course he won at the primaries....

In the meantime Mr. William Hale Thompson decided that he would try to be elected mayor of the city.... [He] thought he could win the nomination if he had the labor vote and the Negro vote. He had the labor vote **cinched** and the speaker was scouting in the Second Ward all summer in the effort to find out who the masses of colored people accepted as leader. He said that he had found that it was not a man but a woman, and that I was that woman.

I inquired what Mr. Thompson proposed to do for colored people in return for their vote....

Mr. Barnett and I both attended [a political] meeting [on the topic] and I was called on to speak.... [I] told them that it would be impossible for me to make any pledge as had been done by the other speakers until I knew what Mr. Thompson's program was with reference to colored people; that I was tired of having white men come out in the Second Ward just before or on election day and buy up the votes of Negroes who had no higher conception of the ballot than to make it a question of barter and sale.

I had always felt that the man who bought votes was just as much to be condemned as the man who sold them, but the world at large did not look upon it in that way. Speaking for those whom I represented, I was sure that we needed greater interest taken in our welfare; that we needed better chance for employment in the city work; and that we especially desired that representation be given us **commensurate** with our voting strength.

Cinched: Made certain; assured.

Commensurate: *Equal in measure.*

Mr. William Hale Thompson was seated in the rear of the room and always wound up his speech by touching upon points made by the speakers of the evening. He came forward and launched at once into an answer to the questions I had asked. Nothing could have been stronger than his endorsement of my views and his promise that if we helped him to win the election he would assure us that nobody would be a better friend to our best interests than he.

That was the beginning of our acquaintance, and for the next six months I threw my heart and soul into the movement. The Second Ward added very largely to the result of securing those one hundred thousand names by the first week in December. We had over twenty thousand pledge cards signed in the Second Ward alone. I sent an appeal to every woman's club and to the heads of other organizations throughout the city assuring them that I believed we had a true friend in this man Thompson and advising them to get pledges for him all over the city. This was done, and when the city woke up William Hale Thompson had two hundred thousand voters pledged to his nomination. This had been accomplished without machine organization and without newspaper assistance.

Things seemed to be going smoothly. It was understood that if Mr. Thompson won, our reading room and social center was to be made an auxiliary of the city, and through our employment agency, colored men were to be given street-cleaning jobs and work in other departments of the city. The Alpha Suffrage Club was the very first organization to endorse Mr. William Hale Thompson for mayor.

Just about the time we felt that the sun was going to shine on our side of the street, and that we were going to have a friend in court who believed in working for the benefit of our people, the regular Republican organization of the city drafted Chief Justice Olson to make the race for mayor against Mr. Thompson. I went at once to Judge Olson's office and asked him why he didn't tell me he was planning to run against Mr. Thompson. I told him I had made speeches all over the town for Mr. Thompson and had gotten everybody I knew to pledge themselves to vote for him; and I had been at this work for six months.

Judge Olson didn't seem to think much of the pledge card idea, and remarked that he had been known to voters for over fifteen years. I did not see how he could overcome Mr. Thompson's lead in three weeks, but I did see that I could make no more speeches for Mr. Thompson and take no more part in his campaign....

[I told a member of Mr. Thompson's campaign office:] "Judge Olson gave me the place I hold in the courts on a silver **salver** and I can neither say nor do anything against him; so I am notifying you that you will have to take my name off your speakers' list. I have told him I don't believe he can overcome the six months' work that we have done for Mr. Thompson in so short a time. My work is done and I can go no further with it."...

Mr. Thompson won at the primary with the help of the Second Ward, and all of our leading politicians proceeded to get on the bandwagon, with the result that William Hale Thompson was elected to the office of mayor with the largest vote that had ever been cast.

It was also the first time that women had voted for mayor. But from the time he was elected, not only Mr. Thompson but all our leading politicians proceeded to ignore those of us who had helped to make it possible for him to realize his ambition. I have been told that when some suggestion was made about keeping a promise to put me on the school board, our men told the mayor that "he didn't owe Mrs. Barnett anything because she did not go with them to the end."

I have also been reminded hundreds of times that I was foolish not to have continued with him, since Judge Olson was not able to keep me in the adult probation office to which he had appointed me. In less than six months after Mayor Thompson's election, I had lost my job. And the Negro Fellowship Reading Room and Social Center had again to fall

Salver: Tray or platter.

back on what we could make from our employment office. (Wells-Barnett in Duster, pp. 345-53)

What happened next...

Wells-Barnett continued to fight for black equality and women's rights for the rest of her life. She worked with reformer Jane Addams to block the segregation of schools in Chicago and helped start the Cook County League of Women's Clubs. She also ran unsuccessfully for Illinois state senator in 1930.

Wells-Barnett made lasting contributions to American history through her work to end both racial and gender prejudices. She is remembered foremost for her leadership of the antilynching campaign and secondarily for her contribution to the women's rights movement.

Did you know...

• At first Wells-Barnett wrote under the pen name "Iola." As her articles on lynching became more well known, she began to give public lectures.

• Wells-Barnett earned $25 per week when she taught at a rural Mississippi school to support her brothers and sisters.

• Abolitionist (antislavery) leader Frederick Douglass wrote the introduction to her most famous book, *The Red Record,* which was published in 1895 and contained statistics concerning lynching.

For Further Reading

Duster, Alfreda M., ed. *Crusade for Justice: The Autobiography of Ida B. Wells.* Chicago: University of Chicago Press, 1970.

Flexner, Eleanor. *Century of Struggle: The Woman's Rights Movement in the United States.* Revised edition. Cambridge, Massachusetts: Belknap/Harvard University Press, 1975.

Harris, Trudier. *Selected Works of Ida B. Wells-Barnett.* New York: Oxford University Press, 1991.

Women's Voices: A Timeline of Events

Sojourner Truth

1790   Judith Sargent Murray publishes "On the Equality of the Sexes."

1792   Mary Wollstonecraft writes *A Vindication of the Rights of Women.*

1819   Emma Willard outlines her plan for female education.

1836   Sarah Bagley leaves home to become a "mill girl."

1836   Ernestine Rose begins to campaign for a married woman's property bill in New York state.

1838   Sarah Grimké composes her *Letters on the Equality of the Sexes.*

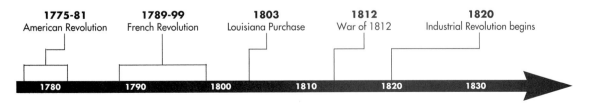

1775-81 American Revolution	**1789-99** French Revolution	**1803** Louisiana Purchase	**1812** War of 1812	**1820** Industrial Revolution begins

1780   1790   1800   1810   1820   1830

1840 Lucretia Mott is not allowed to participate in the World Anti-Slavery Convention in London, England.

1841 Catherine Beecher writes her best-selling book *A Treatise on Domestic Economy.*

1848 Elizabeth Cady Stanton presents her "Declaration of Sentiments" at the first Woman's Rights Convention in Seneca Falls, New York.

1848 Frederick Douglass publishes a supportive article about women's rights in his abolitionist newspaper *The North Star.*

1851 Sojourner Truth delivers her most famous speech "Ain't I a Woman?"

1855 Lucy Stone and Henry Blackwell protest the legal status of married women in their wedding vows.

1861 Julia Ward Howe writes "The Battle Hymn of the Republic."

1865 Thirteenth Amendment abolishes slavery in the United States.

1868 Fourteenth Amendment extends the scope of the Bill of Rights to matters under state jurisdiction.

1869 The National Woman Suffrage Association and the American Woman Suffrage Association are formed.

1869 John Stuart Mill writes *The Subjection of Women.*

1870 Fifteenth Amendment grants voting rights to black men.

1871 Victoria Woodhull argues before Congress that women have the right to vote.

1872 Susan B. Anthony and a group of 16 women are arrested for attempting to vote in the presidential election.

1873 Anthony Comstock helps win passage of the Comstock Law which outlaws the distribution of information about birth control and abortion.

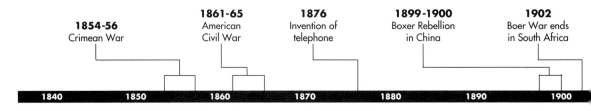

1854-56
Crimean War

1861-65
American
Civil War

1876
Invention of
telephone

1899-1900
Boxer Rebellion
in China

1902
Boer War ends
in South Africa

| 1840 | 1850 | 1860 | 1870 | 1880 | 1890 | 1900 |

1878 Francis Willard conducts her first petition drive for "Home Protection."

1889 Jane Addams organizes a settlement house to help poor immigrants in Chicago.

1896 The Supreme Court's *Plessy vs. Ferguson* ruling establishes the "separate but equal" policy of racial segregation.

1898 Charlotte Perkins Gilmore writes *Women and Economics.*

1900 Carrie Chapman Catt assumes her first term as president of the NAWSA.

1911 A fire at the Triangle Shirtwaist Factory kills 146 female workers.

c.1913 Ida B. Wells-Barnett helps form the first black women's suffrage organization, the Alpha Suffrage Club.

1916 Margaret Sanger opens the first birth control clinic in America.

1916 Emma Goldman is arrested for distributing information about birth control.

1918 Crystal Eastman discusses economic independence and birth control in *The Birth Control Review.*

1920 Nineteenth Amendment grants women the right to vote.

1923 Alice Paul introduces the first Equal Rights Amendment.

1929 Virginia Woolf writes *A Room of One's Own.*

1939-45 Thousands of women go to work in non-traditional factory and military jobs.

1948 United Nations delegate Eleanor Roosevelt plays pivotal role in the adoption of the Universal Declaration of Human Rights.

1953 Simone de Beauvoir publishes *The Second Sex* in English.

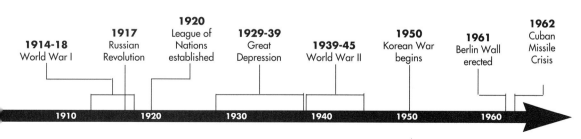

1914-18 World War I

1917 Russian Revolution

1920 League of Nations established

1929-39 Great Depression

1939-45 World War II

1950 Korean War begins

1961 Berlin Wall erected

1962 Cuban Missile Crisis

1910   1920   1930   1940   1950   1960

1954   The Supreme Court rules that segregation in schools is unconstitutional in *Brown vs. Board of Education.*

1963   Equal Pay Act guarantees women "equal pay for equal work."

1963   Betty Friedan writes *The Feminine Mystique.*

1964   Civil Rights Act assures all citizens freedom from discrimination based on race, color, religion, sex, or national origin.

1966   National Organization for Women is founded to promote full equality for both women and men

1968   Pope Paul VI issues *Humanae Vitae* forbidding Roman Catholics from using modern methods of birth control.

1971   Gloria Steinem and other women help create *Ms.* magazine.

1972   Both Houses of Congress pass the Equal Rights Amendment.

1973   The Supreme Court decision *Roe vs. Wade* legalizes abortion.

1982   Phyllis Schlafly's organization "Stop ERA" contributes to the defeat of the Equal Rights Amendment.

1986   Randall Terry starts the pro-life organization Operation Rescue.

1991   Civil Rights Act prohibits sexual harassment on the job.

1993   The Family and Medical Leave Act grants workers unpaid leave to take care of family emergencies.

1994   Shannon Faulkner applies to the Citadel, an all-male military college in South Carolina.

1996   The Virginia Military Institute is ordered to begin accepting women.

1965-75
Vietnam War

1978
Camp David
Peace accords

1980
Solidarity movement
begins in Poland

1989
Tiananmen Square
student
demonstrations

1994
Nelson Mandela
elected president of
South Africa

1970   1975   1980   1985   1990   1995

Photo Credits

Sarah Grimké

The photographs appearing in *Women's Voices: A Documentary History of Women in America* were received from the following sources:

On the cover (from top): Gloria Steinem (**Courtesy of Gloria Steinem. Reproduced by permission.**); Suffragist (**Courtesy of the Cleveland Public Library. Reproduced by permission.**); Ida B. Wells-Barnett (**Courtesy of the University of Chicago. Reproduced by permission.**).

The Granger Collection. Reproduced by permission.: pp. v, 41, 54, 115, 137, 147, 196; **Brown Brothers. Reproduced by permission.:** pp. xi, 121, 132; **Schlesinger Library, Radcliffe College. Reproduced by permission.:** pp. xv, 203; **National Portrait Gallery, Smithsonian Institution. Reproduced by permission.:** pp. 1, 79, 155, 335; **Sargent House Museum, Gloucester, MA. Reproduced by permission.:** pp. 5, 10; **UPI/Corbis-Bettmann. Reproduced by permission.:** pp. 19, 37, 85, 102, 239, 276, 285, 297, 324, 327, 330, 332; **Archive Photos. Reproduced by permis-**

sion.: pp. 23, 30, 75, 118, 155, 191, 232, 335; **Emma Willard School. Reproduced by permission.**: p. 27; **Harriet Beecher Stowe Center. Reproduced by permission.**: p. 33; **Friends Historical Society. Reproduced by permission.**: p. 50; **Courtesy of the Library of Congress:** pp. 63, 72, 82, 89, 130, 141, 159, 171, 209, 224, 339; **AP/Wide World Photos. Reproduced by permission.**: pp. 108, 112, 215, 218, 222, 225, 243, 253, 259, 263, 268, 279, 285, 286, 289, 303, 312, 313, 319; **Courtesy of the University of Chicago. Reproduced by permission.**: 150; **Museum of Textile History. Reproduced by permission.**: pp. 176, 180; **U.S.A.F. Museum. Courtesy of Hugh Morgan.**: p. 200; **Courtesy of the University of Illinois at Chicago, The University Library, Department of Special Collections, Jane Addams Memorial collection. Reproduced by permission.**: p. 206; **Courtesy of the University of Illinois at Chicago, The University Library, Department of Special Collections, Ben Reitman Papers. Reproduced by permission.**: p. 293.

Index

Bold type indicates main documents and speaker profiles

Italic type indicates volume numbers

Illustrations are marked by (ill.)

Lucy Stone

H

Hartford Female Seminary *1:* 2, 29
Haymarket Anarchists *2:* 293, 299, 301
Herland *2:* 202
Hertell, Thomas *2:* 186-187
Heterodoxy *2:* 309
Heyrick, Elizabeth *1:* 51, 52,
Higginson, Colonel Thomas Wentworth *1:* 130, 233; *2:*233
Hogarth Press *2:* 249
Home Protection Manual *1:* **117-125**
How God Is Teaching the Nation *1:* **81-87**
Howe, Julia Ward *1:* 90, **126-135**, 130 (ill.), 132 (ill.)
Howe, Samuel Greatly *1:* 132, 135
Hull House *2:* 172, 205-213
Humanae Vitae *2:* 290, 313

I

I Am Roe: My Life, Roe vs. Wade, and Freedom of Choice *2:* 332
In This Our World *2:* 196
Industrial Reform Lyceum *2:* 183
Industrial Revolution *1:* 126; *2:* 171-172
International Congress of Women *2:* 212
International Ladies Garment Workers Union *2:* 178
International Woman Suffrage Alliance *1:* 138
"Iola" *1:* 154
Iowa Woman Suffrage Association *1:* 141
It Changed My Life *2:* 276, 277

J

Johnson, Lyndon Baines *2:* 221, 319
Johnstown Academy *1:*
Joyce, James *2:* 246

K

Kansas Nebraska Act *1:* 84
Kennedy, John F. *2:* 173, 221, 223

L

The Lady of the Lake *1:* 73
Land Grant Act of 1862 *1:* 8
League for the Rights of Women *2:* 266
League of Women Voters (LWV) *1:* 141, 145, 246
Letters on the Equality of the Sexes *1:* **40-48**

Progress We Have Made *2:* **311-322**
Pugh, Sarah *1:* 51-55

Q

Quakers *1:* 47, 49-56, 58, 107

R

Rationalism *1:* 93
Reconstruction *1:* 87
"Red Emma" *2:* 294
The Red Record *1:* 154
Red Scare *2:* 301
Reminiscences, 1819-1899 *1:* **126-135**
Reproduction *2:* 289-291
The Revolution *1:* 99, 109
Revolutionary War *1:* 1, 4, 100, 139, 186
Red and Blue Ribbon Movements *1:* 119, 120
Rhode Island School of Design *2:* 203
The Rights of Women *1:* **68-73**
Rockford Female Seminary *2:*
Rochester, New York *1:* 68, 73
Roe, Jane *2:* 323-333
Roe vs. Wade *2:* 290, **323-333,** 324 (ill.), 330 (ill.), 332 (ill.)
A Room of One's Own *2:* 226, **248-257**
Roosevelt, Eleanor *2:* 173, **214-224,** 215 (ill.), 218 (ill.), 222 (ill.), 224 (ill.)
Roosevelt, Franklin Delano *2:* 173, 214, 224, 247
Rose, Ernestine L. *2:* 172, **186-194**, 191 (ill.)

S

Sanger, Margaret *2:* 289 (ill.), 290, 294, **311-322,** 312 (ill.), 313 (ill.), 319 (ill.)
Sartre, Jean-Paul *2:* 263, 266
Schlafly, Phyllis *2:* 285
Scott, Sir Walter *1:* 73
The Second Sex *2:* 226, **258-266**
The Second Stage *2:* 276
Second Women's Rights Convention *1:* 75
Selected Correspondence *2:* **228-237**
Selected Writings, 1921, 1924 *2:* **238-247**
Seneca County Courier *1:* 58
Seneca Falls Convention *1:* 68-71, 74
Seneca Falls, New York *1:* 38, 55, 57-67; *2:* 245
Shaw, Anne Howard *1:* 138
Shelley, Mary Wollstonecraft *1:* 18
Shelley, Percy Bysshe *1:* 19

A Vindication of the Rights of Women *1:* 2, **12-19**
Voice of Industry *2:* 183

W

WACS (see Women's Army Corps)
WASPS (see Women's Army Service Pilots)
WCTU (see Women's Christian Temperance Union)
Webster vs. Reproductive Services *2:* 331
Weddington, Sarah *2:* 323-333
Weld, Theodore *1:* 47
Wells-Barnett, Ida B. *1:* 91, **146-154**, 147 (ill.), 150 (ill.)
A Wheel within a Wheel: How I Learned to Ride a Bicycle,
    with Some Reflections by the Way *1:* 125
Who's Afraid of Virginia Woolf *2:* 257
Willard, Emma Hart *1:* 2, 3, **20-28**, 27 (ill.), 29, 65
Willard, Frances E. *1:* 90, **117-125**, 118 (ill.), 121 (ill.)
Wilson, Woodrow *1:* 91
"Winning Plan" *1:* 144
Wollstonecraft, Mary *1:* 1 (ill.), 3, 9, 10, **12-19**, 13 (ill.), 18 (ill.), 19 (ill.)
Woman Citizen *2:* 236
Woman in the Nineteenth Century *1:* 48
Woman Rebel *2:* 290, 312
Woman's Army Corps (WACS) *2:* 199
Woman's National Loyal League *1:* 82
Woman's Peace Party *2:* 303
Women and Economics *1:* 35; *2:* 172, **195-204**
Women's Army Service Pilots (WASPS) *2:* 199
Women's Christian Temperance Union (WCTU) *1:* 117-121, 124
Women's International League for Peace and Freedom *2:* 212, 213, 303
Women's Journal *2:* 236
Women's National Temperance Society *1:* 120
Women's Peace Party *2:* 212
"Women's Rights and Wrongs" *1:* 85
"Women's Strike for Equality" *2:* 276
Women's Temperance Crusade *1:* 120
Woodhull and Clafin's Weekly *1:* 99, 102, 105
Woodhull, Victoria C. *1:* 90, **99-106**, 102 (ill.)
Woodward, Charlotte *1:* 67, 91
Woolf, Virginia *2:* 226, **248-257**, 253 (ill.)
World Anti-Slavery Convention *1:* 38, 49, 50, 57
World War I *2:* 212, 214, 216, 239, 257, 300, 303, 309
World War II *2:* 173, 199, 247, 257

Y

The Yellow Wallpaper *2:* 203